*A London Childhood*

# John Holloway

# *A London Childhood*

With an Introduction by C. P. Snow

Charles Scribner's Sons · New York

*To Emily and Benjamin*

# Contents

# Foreword

I have told this story because for many years I thought my childhood a dull one. Now I think that, at least in retrospect, this is not so. Perhaps nothing is dull. I think the story may be of interest to others, because many others have grown up much the same way. Where this is not quite so, I hope there is still some general interest.

The book goes from 1920 to 1929. That was another world from today. I have not put in all the facts about my childhood, not even all those important to myself; but I have tried to put in what makes a rounded picture, and to be as accurate as I can.

J.H.

# Introduction

John Holloway is one of the three or four most distinguished
critics of his generation in England. He is also a very good poet
—but since English poetry is dominated by academics, writers
outside the academies have ceased to express opinions about it.

That is one reason (a rather oblique one) why it is a pleasure
to express an opinion about his prose writing, where most of
us are not so easily frightened off.

This story of his is a reconstruction of his early childhood,
up to the age of nine. Writing about one's childhood is something of an English passion, like rock climbing, ballroom dancing and solving cross-word puzzles. Sometimes, though not
often, English writers have done it very well. There are two
occupational dangers. One is insipidity. Memory is a tricky
process, and it tends to iron out many of the existential moments: it is a genuine fact that nearly all of us recall the weather
in our childhood as being more unclouded than the meteoro-
logical records will allow. The second danger is lack of individuality. A great deal of most childhoods is more alike than

different: the sensuous details (which are what we recall or try to recall) can be remarkably the same. Sometimes, reading any of the English childhood reminiscences, one feels that one has read them all.

Holloway has coped with both dangers, and achieved a total success. He has avoided insipidity because his mind is strong and he is not afraid of a generalisation. His imagination is concrete: you can smell and feel that house in suburban London: but also he makes it more real, not less, by letting his intellect play round it. We begin to learn just how and why the Holloways were like their neighbours, and how they were different. It is the same hard intelligence, working together with his poet's eye, that gives the book its obstinate individuality. This is not a bit like other reminiscences. You accept—and it is one of the best definitions of a work of art—that everything happened, including the boy himself, exactly *thus*, and could not have been otherwise. There may be a better book of its kind, but if so I don't know it.

I have another motive—subsidiary but not unimportant—why I hope that Americans will read this work. Any country tends to exist, in the minds even of the most sympathetic readers outside it, in stereotype form. The English tend to select, from all the complex of American literature, just those parts which confirm their stereotype. (So do other non-American countries, and the result is curiously unfortunate.) Americans do the same, not quite so grossly, about us. You enjoy reading about a kind of imaginary English upper-class. You are not very happy with the fact, which is true in England as well as in the United States, that the most significant transformation for a hundred years has been the gradual development of a large part of the working class into something with a more comfortable material life and higher expectations. You can't understand modern England without understanding this. It is something the Russians are just getting on to.

Holloway is writing of a family just caught up in—though of course not comprehending—that profound transformation.

He is as accurate in sociological terms as he is in sensuous ones. I can confirm this from my own experience. I was born into a family similar to the Holloways, though in a provincial town, not London, fifteen years before Holloway himself was born. Time and time again, reading his book, I met material details and impressions, not similar to but identical with those that I had known. The interesting thing is that there was half a generation between us. It looks as though the world of everyday, for such families, remained fairly constant for quite a long time. I suspect that it was not until Holloway had grown up that the change became sharply visible: so that anyone writing of such a childhood in the fifties would write an appreciably different book. The world of Holloway's childhood lasted, I should guess, from about 1890 to 1939. He has captured nine years of it, and there it is, preserved in time.

C. P. SNOW

# Chapter one

# A house

'You'll end on the gallows!' my mother said to me once or twice during my childhood, when I had annoyed her more than usual. She was a woman of strong feelings (largely affectionate ones), and when she was heated she spoke with a vehemence and conviction I have not heard since. I am proud of that.

Times have changed a lot since the first nine years of my life, which is what this book is about. Unless I give up my British passport or live too long, my mother's threat is now not likely to come true. But the upshot may be even worse, for all I know. My earliest memory may not augur well for me. It is of a very large and very hot fire.

This earliest memory is of sitting in front of a whitish-red glow, not being able to move, and staring at it for a long time. As I remember it, I feel the warmth. When I described it to my mother—the fireplace, the bars, what the fire was like— she said it must certainly be the fire in the kitchen of Mrs. Newby's house, where she worked as a daily woman until I was about 18 months old. Mrs. Newby was a kind employer, and let her char' bring the apple of her eye, her first-born, her man-child. Words like that were real to my mother. She was a countrywoman by birth, and brought up on the Bible.

At this time we lived at Number 6, Waverley Road, South Norwood. This is now an outer middle suburb of south-east London, but was then almost on the edge of the country. We lived in a small but respectable terrace house. Mrs. Newby lived in Anerley—a long way off, but jobs were hard to find in 1921, and in winter, a job where you could sit your baby in his pram all day, under your eye and by a blazing fire, harder still. That winter there was a long spell of frost, snow, and sleet, then thaw, slush, and freeze again. It was a winter of illness too. But my mother wheeled her pram from South Norwood to Anerley without missing a single day. All the same her shoes leaked. That was what she was like. When she cared, she could do anything, and took no chances.

Later, when I was five or six, we took the same walk once again, so as to have another look at the house. What put it into her mind was the same time of year and the same weather. It was a long way, in ice and slush once more. This time she pushed me in a push-chair. I shall say why she still pushed me. But she hadn't changed. She had a resolve of iron.

I was born in a hospital in Croydon, and brought back to our house when I was a fortnight old. It was in a terrace of six, then there was an alley, and then six more. The other side of the road was the same; except that round the corner, beyond No. 2, was the part of Lonsdale Road that had houses, and at the bottom of our garden were the houses of Brooklyn Road—all of them much like our own. But the part of Lonsdale Road that went across our road and up the slope beyond No. 1—that was all allotments on the nearside, with a big red May tree by No. 1 itself, and on the far side of upper Lonsdale Road, a private kitchen garden behind a grey brick wall with a coping of blue bricks, and some big ashes and elms. So that corner was fairly open, and so was the top of

Waverley Road, where there were more allotments, and the remains of a kitchen garden, now half-derelict, where you could find gooseberries when I was a boy, but sometimes got chased off.

Every detail of a small house grows sharply present to a small boy who lives in it. Ours was red brick, with some yellow plastering round the windows, and it had a three-sided bow-window at the front downstairs, with a little slate roof over it. There was a minute front garden with a short path in ornamental tiles, and a low wall with wrought-iron curly railings, like the front gate. All these details marked it out as a trim little suburban villa. My father was working-class all right, but it wasn't quite a working-class house—all these distinctions and discriminations, though, turning out to be fluid and intricate at any point where you give them a close look. We were at the margin of two big social groups, and exactly what class we were it will take this whole book to convey. From one point of view, it doesn't matter. From another it matters a lot, because it mattered to us.

We didn't have a privet hedge in our front garden, as many of our neighbours did—high, sometimes, so that passers-by couldn't see into the little front parlours—but we did have several shiny green bushes of myrtle, which is much better than privet for finding caterpillars called 'Woolly Bears'. My mother didn't whiten the front step, but she scrubbed it sometimes, and washed down the front path, and polished the brass letterbox. That green front door had two big panels of frosted glass to light the hall and stairs. From the hall you turned left to the front parlour—but I saw little of this room because it was let—or went straight through to the living-room, where indeed we lived, ate, did sewing, ironing and other household jobs. It had linoleum in a faded green pattern, dark wallpaper below the dado, and above it a pinkish-orange paper with a floral pattern in faded stripes. The gas lamp in the middle had a glass over the mantle, and two little black chains hanging down from a bracket, to turn it on and off.

3

Besides the black kitchen range, there was a built-in cupboard where we kept china, clothes, papers, mending and toys. Against the front wall was my mother's piano, with her music in the green plush piano-stool. A kitchen table, four windsor chairs, a folding chair by the fire, a worn armchair in dark brown, a wing armchair in black leather fixed with brass studs, and the 'wireless' cabinet, made a crowded room. The wireless cabinet had to stand in front of the doors in the bow-window and be moved if ever we wanted them open.

The scullery had only a biscuit sink with a brass cold-water tap; a black gas-stove; a zinc 'copper' to boil the washing in; and a chair. It had no daylight except what came through the glass door; this, like the bow-window doors in the kitchen, led to the veranda. We bathed in a zinc bath in the kitchen, which we filled with water we heated in the copper and ladled out with the biggest saucepan. Afterwards, in cold weather, I was wrapped in a towel and run through to dry before the kitchen fire, made very bright specially. You don't easily get such enjoyable baths in a bathroom.

At the back upstairs there were two small bedrooms in green distemper, but one of these was let for most of my childhood. If you leaned out of the window in the other you could see little gardens and roofs and wireless aerials on three sides; but there were one or two lombardy poplars up by that kitchen garden with the gooseberries. You could see them sweeping and heeling over, if it was windy. The front bed-room was big enough to have two windows, and from these you could see almost up to the pillar-box in Chartham Road. There was a big dark cupboard over the stairs. This was where my mother kept her clothes, and inside she had silk and satiny things that were marvellous to touch but you had to be careful not to make them dirty. Her big best coat had a fur collar which was good to stroke as well. She wasn't sure, but she thought it was bear's fur. It had long hair that bristled out if it got wet, and the fog could settle on it in little pearly points.

When it was dry, it was nice to cuddle into on a bus or train. There was really nothing like my mother's bear-fur collar.

To a child, the place he lives in is the heart of the world. No question arises as to why he is there and not somewhere else. But when I look back I can see that there is indeed a question why.

My mother came from Wallingford, a country market-town on the Thames in Berkshire, where her father was head-master of the elementary school and also a noted amateur astronomer and naturalist. He discovered several variable stars and the Colorado beetle, and for many years after his death in 1922, his drawing of this beetle was used in the official Ministry of Agriculture placards. There is a stone plaque about him on the school wall now. He was the younger son of a small Shropshire squire, a man (I never saw him, only his photograph) of generous habits and most noble profile, but no good with money; in the end he lost enough of it to lose his little manor house as well. My mother had seen it as a girl, but it had gone long before my time.

I shall have to say more about my grandmother, not only because that is where the iron in my mother came from, but because her kinsfolk were the only relatives I knew in my childhood. My father's father was a small tenant farmer near Folkestone. I have been told by my mother—he never spoke of these things—that his family had been tenant farmers there since the seventeenth century; but this may have been no more than a family legend. When he was ten he lost his father, and within two years of that, the new manager had got hold of the tenancy of the farm and my father's mother, dispossessed, died like her husband. At twelve or thirteen my father had gone to sea as a ship's boy. Almost everything that belonged to him disappeared in the vicissitudes and constant moving which took place between my tenth and fifteenth year—after the end of this book, and around the time of his death. I do not even have a photo' of him now. But I remember that although he left school so young he could write fluently in a shapely sloping

5

hand. He used to flourish his hand in the air—many people did in those days—before he let the pen touch the paper.

So my father and mother both came from the country, but now we lived in London. Also we lived at a great distance from my father's work, because he worked about 14 miles away, on the north bank of the Thames. In 1922, the year of the publication of *The Waste Land*, my father was one of the crowd that T. S. Eliot saw flowing over London Bridge: he flowed over it daily, not on foot but on his Raleigh bicycle. As for why it was that we lived where we did and he worked where he did, the answer brings in our history over several years, and it is one in which chance, ignorance, inertia, and fear of loneliness play a large part, and reason a small one.

As a young woman, my mother wanted to get away from home. Since her parents would not let her be a singer (which she could easily have done well), she became a nurse. She trained for this at Queen's Hospital in Hackney, for board and lodging and a salary of five pounds a year. George Holloway got a job as a stoker at the hospital shortly before the war of 1914. These two young country people were isolated in London. One had no parents, and the other thought of her mother as fault-findingly hostile, and her father as not much interested. That neither had a penny only made them depend more on each other. When they were free, they sat on a seat in the local park. My mother has told me how they shared the warmth of the sun, seeing green leaves or the buds breaking, looking at the flowers or listening to the sparrows. They shared the simplest joke or a little human gaiety. Although they were barely any longer in their early twenties, it seems that neither had been in love. My mother had been attached to a young man—no, to one and then to another young man— down in the country: but this had been squashed, like so much else, by my grandmother. Neither my mother nor my father had at this time the faintest idea of what life could offer or what it could threaten. My mother often said that later herself. They were naive and a little sentimental. This went in my father with bluffness and brusquerie, and in my mother with a great deal of sharp perception and dry wit. They both, even much later, when I was old enough to take this in, used to say their best things quite without knowing how good they were.

They married shortly after the outbreak of war, because my father was going away. First he was in the 'Rough-Riders' (the City of London Yeomanry) and for a long time there was a large photograph of him, looking unusually spruce and handsome, with the beautiful black horse that he rode so naturally and so well. My mother was proud of this; it was another shared country thing. They married because my father's having to go meant that each of these two country people in the metropolis faced the kind of isolation they had known before they met. In saying that, I am again repeating how things were explained to me. One must also remember that this was London early in 1915.

My mother wanted to go on as a nurse at the hospital, but although her husband was away (at first in the Dardenelles) she was not wanted because she was married. I suppose nurses had to be thought to be virgins. So she worked for about six months as a private nurse in a large house in its own grounds in South Norwood. This house, called 'Norhurst', I often glimpsed, through its big trees, during my childhood; the bus I went to school on ran up South Norwood Hill along the edge of the grounds. The family was a rich and cultivated family of German Jews who had emigrated from Germany a good time before the war, and now called themselves by the name of Frost. My mother's work was to look after Mrs. Frost, who fell short of vigorous health, and thought herself an invalid. But during this period (as my mother used to explain to me) anti-German feeling was growing so bitter that in the end the tradesmen would not deliver food, and police wandered about the grounds at night looking for chinks of light at the windows. It was thought that the Frosts were signalling, with their chinks of light, to the zeppelins. In the end there came a time when the family either moved right away or was interned, I don't know which. I think Mr. Frost was interned.

My mother then got a job working on munitions at the firm of Gillet and Johnson on the Norwood outskirts of Croydon; and lodged—here the house of my childhood came into the story—at 6 Waverley Road with Mr. and Mrs. King. Mr. King was a recruiting sergeant—I think he was billeted at home though—and Mrs. King was a noisy, loquacious, good-hearted Irishwoman whom I can just remember. Towards the end of the war Gillet and Johnson began to give people the sack; so, either just after, or just before she got it, my mother found work with a small firm in South Norwood, run by a Mr. Tinsley. It made bits and pieces for the very early days of radio—'wireless' we called it, and this is the word that still comes most naturally to my lips.

My father miraculously came out of the army unhurt, save for a shrapnel scar down the front of his leg, and gas. This was after three years on the Western Front in the machine-gun corps (the cavalry, of course, being soon disbanded). He went back to his old job at Queen's Hospital, came to live with my mother at Waverley Road, bought the three-speed Raleigh bicycle without which my childhood must have been quite different from what it was, and began to cycle daily to work.

On the whole, the Holloways and the Kings got on well. Mr. King, whom I can remember from calls he paid us during my own childhood later, was a dignified, slow-spoken man: I suspect he may have thought it part of his dignity to be tolerant of this entertaining, improbable, slightly crazy pair. His heavy black civilian shoes were polished to a high glitter on the toes, and left dubbed with dressing, but not polished at all, at the heels. 'A good soldier never looks behind', he used to say about this. How many bars, I later wondered, had he held his own in for a minute with this witticism?

In the end, the usual thing happened. The Kings left, and their lodgers the Holloways took over the house. This means of course the tenancy: the landlord was someone whom we saw only once or twice during my whole childhood, and the rent, thirteen shillings each week, was collected each Monday by a Mr. Bull, who came with his book under his arm. Then, in the course of time, we began to acquire lodgers of our own. Soon, the depression of 1920 set in. In the 1920s, there were often so many houses being let or sold, that the agents' boards could look like flags on a jubilee, they were so thick down the street. My father and mother could have got another house much nearer to Hackney, had they wanted; but South Norwood, at this time, was on the very edge of London. From here, a short bus-ride would get them into the country; and later I must write at more length of the ways in which they contrived to get back to what both belonged to at heart all their lives.

But something like the countryside was no more than a stone's throw from the door. I think Waverley was an unmade road when they went there, and even at the beginning of my childhood. Archer Road, the prolongation of it into town, remained unmade and gravelly until after we left in 1929. Upper Lonsdale Road was also unmade. At the bottom of Waverley Road, a broad green path ran through countrified allotments to Love Lane, which was a cycle-path, with tarmac or broad flagstones here and there, and turned into a narrow road with a row of cottages at one end. Otherwise it ran between lush hawthorn hedges, so white with blossom in spring that the branches seemed to sag. Before the houses, there was just one gas lamp in its whole length. Beyond lay the almost empty cemetery, and the lonely sewage farm with its single footpath to the village of Elmers End. To me as a child, the journey across the sewage farm seemed immense and daunting, but in the year I was born, it would have been barely more than a mile this way from our house to fields, woods, a country stream and herds of cows.

From time to time, my mother used to suggest moving nearer to my father's work; or ask if he wanted to, and say she didn't mind. But he would never hear of it. Partly this was because, less intelligent and at heart much more a country-man than she, he dreaded change and the unknown with a kind of surly, angry bewilderment. Partly, it was because he liked the traces of country in where we lived. But the real fact is, neither of them had the knowledge or the powers needed to weigh up their position. They could not have cal-culated that if they moved to north London, they might find as much country, and more, at less than half the distance from Hackney. My father's work-mates all lived in the slums at walking distance from the hospital. They would have given us no advice about country. Up to when I was seven or eight, we had no map of London. If it had entered my parents' minds that they might live, say, at Edmonton, they were in no position to hear about houses to let, still less to visit them if they had heard, and still less again to move to one if they had found one. My mother could screw herself up to almost any-thing if it really had to be done; but that is another thing. My father would have become unsure, nervous, and therefore aggressive, if he had as much as gone into the enquiry office of a firm big enough to move a household across London in those days. In a minute or so he would have found some excuse to bluster his way out again. People whose walk of life was like ours were caught in a web. They could not so much as see the strands of it, but it circumscribed all they did. Everyone is in a web of some sort or another; but not all webs have the same tight grip.

There is also another side to all this: one reason why my parents did not try to change their situation was that in some ways it was good. By his job, as by his powers, my father stood far below the top of the working class: but because, in the upheaval of the war, we had come by the house, because we took two lodgers, because my father had the stamina for those bicycle rides, and also because of another thing—I shall come to it—we maintained ourselves in a house, a street, a locality, well above the bottom of the middle class. Coventry

Road we should have thought an impossible place to live in: it was a working-class slum. But we didn't live in Apsley Road, or even Harrington Road, either. Even as a small boy I was conscious of the slightest distinctions between the streets —whitened steps, bow-windows, frosted glass in the front doors, fences, iron railings, front gardens, hedges, golden not green privet, a myrtle bush, and a great deal else. Maybe I was born a snob: but I think it was because I detected the constantly varying nuances in how my parents spoke of these places. Waverley Road was, in a grotesque sense of course, really rather select. From our front windows you could almost see across to the houses of Chartham Road, where the elderly Miss Tinsley now lived. She was sister to my mother's ex-employer. We spoke of her in tones of deep respect. The houses in Chartham Road were bigger than ours; but I noticed with interest, as a small boy, that their ornamental iron railings and front gate were almost the same as ours.

My father would never have given up his job. These were the 1920s. 'Lose my job' was the great horror. He, and I think some others, had had a sort of assurance that while the hospital itself went on, they would not be turned off: and nothing would have induced him to work for a South Norwood employer who would have been a stranger, for whom he would have had no record of service and no meaning. He dreaded the sea of joblessness: rightly, though I cannot say wisely, for he had no familiarity with politics, unionism or any such thing. I don't think he belonged to a Union: in any case, as he helped to keep the hospital warm, he wasn't in the General Strike (which I knew about simply through going to school or on the back of a lorry). I don't think he was ever in a strike. His fear of joblessness was intuitive and primitive. We used to see the unemployed men—grey figures, their clothes were always grey, or else greyish-blue—with caps and scarves and their hands in their pockets for the cold—standing in little knots outside the Labour Exchange in Coventry Road (where the crop-headed boys lived), which stood right next to St. Mark's Church; where my mother took me, at the age of six or seven, to hear Stainer's *Crucifixion*.

But there was another reason why my father would not have changed: 'the mates', as he called them. His real job was to stoke the hospital furnaces, though in the course of years he became something of a general handyman in the hospital, and did jobs like painting and distempering and putting up shelves. He had three or four companions that he liked a lot; so much so that in 1928, when he was offered a transfer to be stoker and handyman in the hospital's convalescent home at Little-hampton, near Bognor, he refused. It would have meant more money, easier work, and living perhaps five minutes' walk from work in what was then almost a village. Two miles away, over the heath, lay a big and at that time deserted beach. He might be alive today if he had gone. He refused partly through liking the company of 'the mates' and partly also, I think, from a kind of loyalty to them which made him unhappy at the thought of having it so much more cushy than them.

Naturally enough, I saw them almost never. They were all so far away, it was another world. Bill Hawkes, a tall, heavily-built man with a red face and rounded features, his short, dark-brown hair flat down on a big round head, called on us once, quite unexpectedly, with some item of news. His open-neck cream shirt and brown tweed jacket gave him a great air of easy superiority in my eyes. I think in fact that he was the senior hand, though not the foreman.

Apart, perhaps, from when I was too young to know— I think my mother took me shortly after I was born, to show to one or two of her special friends, like Nurse Hayes—I went only once to Queen's Hospital.

I was about seven when we went. I can't remember the journey, but I can remember that it finished up with a ride on a tram, and I can remember very clearly the impression I had of that part of London. It was blackness. It seemed as if there were very wide streets, perfectly straight and at right angles

to each other, and very tall buildings; but the same everywhere, so that from outside, each block seemed like a single
giant building in a very large cube. And everything was black.
But I was taken inside the hospital and here of course it was
not black but clean. It had long warm corridors, going all
ways and seeming endless (it was by far the largest building I
had ever been into). It was painted in cream and a pale bright
green, and from time to time we stopped and I was told that
my father had decorated this room, or put up these shelves, or
whatever it was.

Then I was taken to see the furnace-room. I had kept on
asking for this. It was down a flight of stone steps: a long,
narrow, half-basement room, with three furnaces on the right-
hand side as you looked in. To the left were the coal-bunkers.
I think they must have been filled through chutes in the wall.
The room was hot, the heat struck you suddenly and roughly
as you came down the steps. They took me down in front of
the great round iron faces of the furnaces and said did I want
to see inside, see them do the stoking? Of course I said yes. The
furnace door was really small, not much bigger than the door
on our kitchen range. I was surprised. Yet before they opened
it they were careful to make me stand back, and to make sure
I would stand still. When they clanged open the door I just felt
it suddenly warmer, but then, stooping a little, the radiant heat
struck my face like a quick hard blow. There inside, I saw the
face of the fire, raking gently backward, very smooth and flat,
and a fierce yellow. I had no idea any burning thing could be
so big. From the burning came a little noise I had not expected,
like a man's deep gasp, but quiet and very sustained. The long-
handled shovel, shaped a little like a spoon, went in and turned
over, and the big black heap of coal in it seemed to melt away.

Two of the three furnaces were kept at work all the time,
and there were three men working at once to stoke them. I
think they put fuel on every ninety seconds. They did not
have any kind of break during their eight hours, but they
could eat at their sandwiches in gaps between shovelling, or

perhaps rest a little. These men were proud of their skill with the fires, and how they knew the way to keep them smoothly and evenly burning on as little coal as could be.

We ourselves did not depend wholly on the very small wages my father earned for stoking the furnaces. Besides our two lodgers, we had a little money from short articles which my mother wrote. They were modest pieces. At one time she did notes on herbal flowers for the *Nursing Mirror*. Largely, she could write these out of her own head, just recalling the things she had learnt from the country-folk as a child. But she also drew an illustration, each week, of the plant she was writing about; and these were published too. I remember a really good drawing of that hairy plant the Borage. She drew very slowly, with great patience. As a matter of fact, my father could draw much better; for many years we had on the wall a water-colour he did of two parrots, which he copied from a Sharpe's toffee tin, and which was far more subtly and harmoniously done than the original. Still, paper is subtler than tin.

My mother stayed up far into the night to do those pieces, sitting at the kitchen table after the fire had gone out. Once I woke up and came down and found her at it. That was about one o'clock.

But we also had something else much more substantial: what was for us a quite sizeable sum that my mother had saved out of her wages on munitions. She kept this in a deposit account in a quiet little branch of the Westminster Bank near Penge West Station. We used to go and collect the interest sometimes. It was a long walk. He was a well-spoken, friendly man, that cashier, and I used to wish we saw him more often. Then we began to, because my father found out about this money. Up to then it was what had bought me my warm clothes and dry shoes and so on. Now, not unreasonably, he wanted his share; and as I got bigger I suppose I also got more expensive. Little by little my mother ate into the principal. The walks to Penge got more frequent and less joyful. When I was seven or eight it had all gone, and this made a difference.

## Chapter two

# A large-hearted boy

When I was about six and a half, a school doctor with a wrinkled round face and a tooth-brush moustache and a brown suit and very clean hands gave me a medical examination; and having listened to my heart through a stethoscope, he declared it was enlarged, and I had a heart murmur. My mother's knowledge as a nurse and her country dreads and superstitions came together—not for the only time—and she was alarmed. The people at school seemed to care too, and I was not allowed to play rough games in the playground for a year or so—Bertie Crouch the gardener's son chased me vigorously on one occasion, and ended (as such boys could) sliding stylishly up to the fence on his hob-nail boots, only to find Miss Martin standing there waiting to give him a ticking-off for chasing a boy with a weak heart. I was also not allowed to go swimming, later on in my schooldays, and at that time I used to walk to the swimming baths with the others, but then just hang about. It was the same when we marched in a crocodile down to the recreation ground to play football; and this too was why I got partly wheeled when we went back to have a look at the Newby's house. Of course I walked a great deal, but I used to get wheeled as well.

The chief effect of what the doctor said, though, was that after a very long time—quite enough for it to have come too late, I should think, had it really been needed—a camp bed turned up in the school, and I had to take part in lessons, for an hour a day after lunch, lying flat out on it at the front of the class. I suppose I was the star pupil at that little suburban church school (it was in Upper Norwood, a much more stylish part than ours). I hope they would have been at the same trouble for a very dull boy. They might.

Certainly it sounds a bit disagreeable. I viewed the long-awaited coming of that bed with strong dislike, because I thought I should be teased about it by the other children, and somehow treated more severely otherwise by the teachers, to make up. It did not work out like that. My classmates thought it great fun on the first day, but they were full of kindness about it, didn't tease me, and in fact most of them kept off the whole subject. Soon it became a matter of routine, and no one took any notice. Now, I see it as one more sign of how easily children behave in a grown-up way if you give them a chance. It also says a good deal for the teachers in that serene and gentle school, so different from the one I went to when I was eight.

I must have seemed a clever boy to the teachers, because it was decided that I should be entered for the Victoria Scholarship at 'The Whitgift'—the well-known public school in Croydon where I could have gone (to the preparatory department at first no doubt) as a day-boy. I learned that there was just one Scholarship open for boys like myself, and I can remember thinking about this with—in a childish sense—much misgiving. It was easy to see that I was the top child in my class, but I was not at all the sort of child who thinks that if a distinction exists, it is for him. I didn't in the least see myself as bound for the Victoria Scholarship. Anyway, Croydon for me meant simply the big High Street and the crowds, and wandering about in the toy department at Kennards. At the same time I was vaguely aware that Mr.Cartwright the headmaster, and the others too, were being quite business-like and serious about it all. I now see that they thought they were going to get that Victoria Scholarship for their little school. Reviewing it all now, I suppose they were quite possibly right. Not that it matters much. Scholastic ability seems to me to go with car-performance or wealth, not beauty or goodness. It is just a possible means to good things, not a good thing in itself. As such it is rather a bore.

Anyhow, Mr. Williams, a young and (as I found him) rather forbidding man, prim and severe, began to coach me in Latin from a slim book with 'Elementa Latina' in red down the spine. My mother tried to help me, but really all she could do was hold the book and hear me say 'to or for a table' and 'with, by or from a table' and 'Caesar kills Balbus' and things like that. 'O table' made us laugh and mystified us a bit: my mother had done some Latin at school, but 'O table' had mystified her then, and the years hadn't changed things. However, in those days the idea that the text book might ask one to learn wrongly, just didn't exist. To learn Latin was to learn *Elementa Latina*. I don't think, even now, that there's any harm in this—for the bookish ones. When you're young and quick, it doesn't much matter whether your lessons have been rationalized and streamlined by someone clever and up-to-date, or not. The great thing is to be learning and learning.

Yet I don't believe I did very well with my Latin. A restricted family background—however affectionate, however co-operative—hinders a child's academic success because it leaves him doubting its value and unclear as to its upshot. My slim blue book had to be learned alone, and doing homework while all the others were playing, in order to go I didn't really know where or why. In the end, my Latin and all the rest came to nothing, and I got on by another road in another place.

When I was ten and a half—this takes me to a period outside this book, but I shall touch on it for a minute so as to put these years in perspective—I went by myself to watch motor-cycle racing on a grass track near Biggin Hill. I thought about where I should get the most exciting views, and I got the answer just right. But ignorance of one important fact caused me trouble. I had been once or twice to the Crystal Palace to watch dirt-track racing with my father: but this had not taught me that amateurs, racing on grass, can leave the track and plough through the spectators. My choice of a point of vantage set me—it would, of course—exactly where this was to happen. I still have a vivid mental picture of the valves of a motor-bicycle threshing up and down very close to my face. I picked myself up, realized I was hurt but could run, and set off at a desperate top speed for the tall thick hedge. Here I proposed to hide, and use my handkerchief to deal with the fact that I was bleeding. As I grew aware of the fact that I was really bleeding quite a lot, from the back of my hand, I was intercepted by a St. John's Ambulance man, and in a moment was sitting on the ground, being bandaged up—in several places, not just my hand where a small artery had been severed (I have a slight scar still). I was surrounded of course by a tight-packed circle of gawping strangers. Later I was driven home in a private car, and I think this was the first time I went in one.

Anyhow, all this, though it did me no harm save that it disfigured one finger-nail for a few years, meant that I had to go for the 11+ medical examination swathed in bandages on my leg, arm and face. We were left to think that if I failed to pass, I failed in the whole exam, but I suppose this was simply one more case of how the ignorant and naive are left to suffer; no doubt it was an examination which merely ensured that if a boy needed treatment he got it. I was very much afraid I should fail because of my bandages, though I saw the point when the doctor grinned and said 'that sort of thing makes no difference to me.'

Well, the doctor read about my enlarged heart and old murmur in his records, and seemed to take it all seriously. He listened to me, up and down, and more than once, through his instruments. Then he said: 'there's nothing wrong with this boy's heart'; and since my mother of course felt that a county school doctor would know more than a primary school one, she was very pleased. But then he went on to declare that there never had been anything wrong with it either. So in all probability the trouble and effort of those years of no games and the camp bed had been wasted. I am grateful for the error, though. I once had the makings of a good wing or wing-three-quarter footballer, a Machiavellian bowler of left-hand breaks, and a lively slosher as batsman. But by the time I had this medical examination, and could 'do games' like everyone else, I'd learnt better ways of using my time than running after balls; and never really got drawn in.

The idea that I had a weak heart made my mother do more than ever for me. She used always to meet me for the meal in the middle of the day (at that time there were no meals served at school). Sometimes we used to go to a cook-house in a little row of shops on the way to the Round Pond and the Rookery at Streatham. The cheapest two-course meal was eleven pence, and the dearest was one-and-four. We were served by a burly blue-eyed man, his fair hair greying, his apron very white, his hands very washed. He cooked and served and did everything, with his wife a very small figure in the back of the shop. He made fine apple pies, which had cloves in them. I had never tasted clove in apple before.

But paying this much for dinner (as we called it) was rather a lot for us; so usually my mother used to bring a meal in her shopping basket, and we would take it into Grange Wood Park and eat it there. The Park had once been the grounds of a big house: we wandered about the stables once or twice, but the big Victorian house we didn't go inside. There were long, dark holly-drives, and what was almost a holly wood, with the trees big enough for it to be clear underneath them, and we sheltered there once or twice from the rain. Also there was a big shelter, made of pine-trunks and thatched. We sheltered there too, several times: it seemed to rain quite often on the days we took our lunch in the Park, and we had to watch our shoes for the wet: mine because they were small, and my mother's because they were poor. Besides the hollies, there were many sweet-chestnut trees; and we often tried to find some that we could eat, but never did.

My mother used to bring fine lunches. She must have spent the morning on them. Above all she would bring ginger puddings, which I adored, in our white pudding-basin wrapped in an old towel to keep warm. For me it was like magic, on a cold day, to sit on one of the green slatted benches, and see the towel and then the pudding-cloth come off, and the steam from the pudding fume up. We had plates and spoons, and cornflour sauce and all sometimes: she could see how much this dish made me happy, and she brought it over and over. It was while eating one of these puddings that I first heard the cuckoo: and the note of the cuckoo and the taste of ginger still go together in my mind. Several times we ate our lunch there in the snow, and sharp, sharp cold. When I think of these times I recall the bite of the cold and the hot taste and warm colour of the pudding together too. There were jays there as well as the cuckoo; strange and exotic they seemed, and slow-moving —as indeed they are. Once, but only once, we saw the cuckoo that we so often heard. This bird seemed mysterious to me, so often close yet so seldom seen. I thought about the cuckoo a little as one might about the phoenix, as if there were only one.

My mother had what at any rate used once to be the country feeling for all living creatures: whether you like them or not, and quite probably you do not, they are immediately and vividly *there*, as much as any human being. After the time of this book, and when I was nine and we lived further out and in a more rural place, she once woke me up in the middle of the night, and what she wanted me for was to look through her bedroom window at the garden—it was mauve with the moonlight, I see it still—and listen to a nightingale, sitting on a bush not twenty feet away. It meant so much to her, partly because it was the first nightingale she had heard for twenty years: the move we had made was bringing back to her some of the things she had lost when she lost the world of her childhood. I shall never cease to be grateful for how she did such things for me: she was more romantic than was good for her—or others—but the simple fact is that it is better to care than not to care.

She passed caring on to me. I can remember when I was just seven, wanting to go into the road near my school and rescue a toad from the traffic: it must have been a busy time of day, because for once there was a lot of traffic. I was forbidden to do this by an older boy, who was a prefect or something. This was almost the only time he spoke to me, but the thing left its mark so that I can remember his name (it was Nunn) as I remember no one else's at that school except that of my first girl, Beryl Rowe, and Bertie Crouch. I was in deep distress about the toad, which I had to watch lumbering and hopping helplessly. My mother appeared on the scene at just that moment, and Nunn felt his job was finished, and sheered off. I don't think my mother rescued the toad either; in fact, I think it rescued itself.

It's not true that I remember only those names, because I remember another. There was a boy called Mills. He wore grey flannel shorts and a grey jersey, which he had inside his trousers and his belt. Miss Jarvis, who was a fussy old marm we all thought, told him one day that this wasn't the right way to wear his jersey, and that he was to wear it outside. And he blushed as he began to pull it out, and said in shame, 'it's all holes, Miss'. So she told him to put it back again.

Bertie Crouch's father was a gardener, and they lived in a cottage down the road and the steep hill to Grange Wood Park: I think he was a gardener in the Park somewhere, but we never knew him, and he was certainly not the gardener in a blue serge apron that my mother used to chat with sometimes. Higher up the hill were two other houses. At the top, on the corner by the main road, was a house in Victorian grey brick, almost a Cottage *orné*, that had been the lodge to Grange

Wood Manor in its heyday. Mrs. Brown lived here. She was a portly, stately woman well into middle age, and had grey hair, almost golden-white in fact, that she did loosely, in a bun. She and my mother became good friends and we used to go there and have tea after our lunch, or tea after school at four: but then we were usually soon shepherded off, because Mr. Brown was coming in. Sometimes the adults played whist, a game my mother used to like a good deal, and played at home with my father; using a dummy hand, if someone else could be found for a third (they never had four). At the Browns they also taught me to play rummy, and on one occasion must have amused themselves by letting me win, because I won for a long time and got very excited. 'I'm determined to win!' I kept saying. My mother was quite cross for the rest of the day, once we left. It must have been silly and troublesome of me; though if you keep it to yourself, the sentiment is all right.

Just down the slope from Mrs. Brown's house was a small white house. It stood inside its own oak fence all round, and house, garden, fence and all stood inside a little wood that ran down the hill. This was where Mrs. Field lived. I think we went into her house only once or twice. It was full of copper ornaments, all spaced out, and white inside the way it was outside. Mrs. Field was a blonde, she had hair of a deep red-gold, which she brushed very smooth. Her husband was a good-looking man, smooth and confident-voiced and breezy. He was nice to us but didn't lose any time. I saw later that the Fields were really much above the Browns in their ways and their aspirations. Those copper pots, that golden hair, and Mrs. Field usually seemed to wear a black costume in her little white house. Perhaps they were (in the 1920s) just a bit 'arty'. If so, it was a long while before I touched against that world once more.

School stopped at midday and did not begin again until two, and so we had a long lunch-time, and it seemed in a way like the third part of the schoolday, along with the morning and the afternoon, instead of just a gap between them. It was

on the way home after school, though, that I used to see my
other favourite part of that higher, up-the-hill world of
schooldays. Halfway down South Norwood Hill—and immediately beyond the point where Beryl and her mother,
walking home with us, would turn off right along White
Horse Lane, so it fitted in very well—we could turn off to the
left and go down Woodvale Avenue. At the time, this was a
private road; 'not adopted', they used to call them. It had just a
gravel surface, and there were almost no houses in it, at least
that I remember. But on either side was a long line of chestnut
trees, not the high but the wide, spreading kind, that met overhead in the middle, and made the road twilit and mysterious in
my eyes. In autumn the colours were first very rich and warm,
then deeper and blacker as the autumn rain soaked into the
leaves thick underfoot. They used to be so thick that I found as
a child my feet lost touch with the ground; even when I
kicked the leaves up, a cloudy puff at every step, I would still
be walking on the lower leaves beneath.

It was really no further home this way, but slower because of
the walking and because there was more to stop and look at.
Sometimes also my mother would run into the gardener from
Norhurst; because this road ran along the edge of it. He was a
shortish man, but powerfully built, with a masculine, bony
face, and wore a grey cap he pulled well down. He spoke in a
slow, heavy way; looking back at him now, I think he found
my mother attractive, and since he wasn't the flirtatious kind
it came out in this wooden doggedness. They talked about the
big house and the old days and old people there. He'd not
worked at Norhurst when my mother had, but they had many
experiences and memories that linked and fitted in to each
other, and sometimes they talked a good while. Once or twice
the three of us took shelter in the big stables while it rained.
They were ordinary Victorian stables with the gently sloping
roofs and wide eaves and large flat wall-spaces of their time;
but set deep in the chestnuts, with a worn court of granite
blocks, and the great doors and gateways that a stable has to

23

have. These stables had a poetry about them. Dimly, they opened up a large country to my imagination; I took in the fact that these great rambling buildings were simply where the horses had lived, were set in some corner, right away from the house itself.

One result of my alleged weak heart was that in my second year at school I used to stay in the classroom during play-time. Miss Bailey, the five-year-olds' teacher, a dear, kind grey-haired woman who is, I think, the only person in my whole childhood whom I can look back on with completely happy feelings, and Miss Martin, the young, be-spectacled teacher for the six-year-olds, who was also a nice woman though a bit sharper, used to make tea together in a small blue-enamelled teapot, and sometimes gave me a cup. Sometimes a handful of other children would stay in too, and each of us would get a biscuit. (How generous those two dear women were! Six or seven biscuits, a good few times a week, must have shown against their wages.) Once, when they were out, and with strong feelings of guilt, I took a second one, of a kind I specially liked: though seeing, really, that my being in a way a special case, down on my camp bed (or supposed to be, anyhow), would soften their disapproval but didn't make it right. Back came Miss Martin and someone told her what I'd done. She did disapprove: 'You know what *that* is, don't you!' she said to me. I filled with horror. I knew only one crime worse than stealing, and that was murder. Perhaps I'd end up just where my mother said. 'Yes, miss, greedy,' said Bertie Crouch at top speed. He was glad to get one in. Miss Martin hesitated, and then let it go. I wasn't taken in, though I think I was half taken in. It was my first experience, so far as I recall, of people with a vocabulary of grey words only, for a world full of white and black facts.

All Saints was a church school, and at the age of six we spent a good deal of time every morning learning the catechism. One phrase in the catechism gave me much food for thought. This was about 'doing my duty in that station in life in which it hath pleased Providence to call me'. The teachers explained this, in those far-off days, much as I suppose it was explained when it was adopted under Queen Elizabeth: rich were rich, and poor poor, and you accepted your lot. For my part, however, I resented the phrase, because it seemed to challenge my right to try for the Victoria Scholarship. I thought a good deal about this. I can't remember if I reached for myself, or got by asking a teacher, the conclusion that it might be exactly to this Victoria Scholarship that in my case Providence was pleased to issue its call; but certainly I was aware (in retrospect this surprises me) that if so, a lot more followed, in that anyone could pull himself up to anywhere, provided only that his boot-strings were long enough. I didn't, of course, so much as glimpse the logic behind all this: only, that what had seemed easy to understand very well was something you couldn't understand at all, once you really tried.

Natural enough, though: an only child, very close to a most intelligent mother, and talking to her all day long, I was in some degree a little adult. I really could think: though I hadn't the least idea of either the rareness of that, or its value. 'Why did God save us by turning himself into just a poor carpenter's son?' Miss Martin asked us once. Couldn't he, her point was, have done it without quite so deep a descent . . . ? Nobody could say, till I realized more or less, that if you did this you showed you thought it was all right to be a poor carpenter, you weren't stand-offish or snobbish. So I said, more or less, that it was because God loved us such a lot and wanted to share it. Miss Martin, impressed, asked if someone had told me that, or I'd guessed it for myself. But alas! It was to be at least ten years before I got my values right in this matter. At six, it seemed to me nothing to have guessed, and much to my credit to have learnt from a sound authority. So I said my mother had told me, which was altogether a lie. It looks as if my intelligence was stronger than my moral sense, though not strong enough. This may still be so.

# Chapter three

# Ill, cold and warm

I was seven in August 1927, and almost on my birthday I got whooping-cough. I must have had this disagreeable illness rather badly, and I was not able to go back to school until late in September. Since I was slow in getting better, my mother thought I needed fresh country air. Her way of getting this was a mark not only of how she loved her man-child, but also of that iron in her which I did not understand at the time.

My father worked a seven day week for three weeks in the month. When he worked 'six to two' he would be away in the day; when he worked the night shift he would usually go to bed after breakfast; and when he worked two to ten he would often stay in bed late. So there would be just the two of us. Every single day while I was getting better from whooping-cough, my mother would make up a picnic lunch, wrap me up, and put me into my push-chair; which I could still sit in, though I was getting big for it, and I can remember the feel of it on my arms, and how my feet fitted firmly now on the foot-board which bent my knees up. Then she pushed me to the

Shirley Hills, the nearest stretch of high ground with something of the country about it.

With my mother moving at a quick pace, for we had a long way to go (well over two miles) we would go down lower Albert Road, along the triple line of pines at the edge of the sewage farm, then to the bottom of Portland Road, where it was always busy, then over the high railway bridge, with a long approach up and down, where for the first time you could see the country in the distance. Then we skirted a park and turned into Shirley Road. This began with little new houses, but we were wheeling through the hedges before we came to the junction by the luxury hotel (set out of sight in a wood), where the road dipped down and at last began to go steadily uphill for a long way. This was the beginning of Shirley village, with a black weatherboard sweetshop, and a windmill, starkly near to the road, which didn't go round any more, but was kept in trim order by the man who lived in it. Now the houses were all different and individual. They were set back from the road, and with trim clipped hedges, very green. Some were more cottages than houses. My mother went more slowly, and I could hear her laboured breathing as she pushed. It was a long hill.

In the end we would come to the Common, on the right; on the other side were big private woods of oak and pine, and the last few houses, with a small rural café. Like all such places, it was quite empty and deserted on weekdays: it would even be a long time before the old man came through from the back to see what you wanted. This was another weatherboarded place, just one storey high. The windows were small, and it had green-painted benches, and tables covered with white American cloth, like our own table. We never saw any cars, or perhaps just one, the whole time we were going up the hill. So it would be very quiet in that little café; in fact, it would be absolutely silent for a long time at a stretch. Or if we took shelter there from the rain, we could hear nothing but the rain beating on the roof, very close above our heads.

27

The Hills themselves were high enough to give a view right across Norwood to the next hills, nearer to London, that the Crystal Palace stood on. It surprised me, even then, how much what I knew was all houses could look like all trees. On the south side, at the top of the rise, dense belts of woodland stretched behind long runs of oak paling; and we never saw across to the real countryside beyond. It was the grounds of Addington Palace, some of it by this time become a golf course, that lay behind those long oak fences. I knew there was somewhere called 'Bishop's Walk' there, and the bishop's palace; and in my mind's eye I had an image of the bishop, crozier, mitre, satiny white vestments and all, among the trees.

We used to take a ball in the stiff round shopping basket with the lunch in it. I held this on my knee, or my mother used to prop it on the footboard, with me holding it, when I got tired of that. But we didn't play ball for long. I used to like brushing my feet through the deep carpet of pine-needles, and sometimes climbed the trees, not very high. There was one pine that divided into two very close to the ground, I specially liked to climb it. But it was not always easy to find the place you wanted, because the Shirley Hills are a series of parallel ravines, all running northward, side by side, from the high ground at the top, and all much like each other; though my impression was that as you went further on from home, the ravines grew deeper and steeper. The bottom of each was filled with big pebbles, greyish-white and rounded, that made a harsh crunching noise, quite loud, if you ran on them. Sometimes there were pebble-runs, almost like little screes, at the sides of these ravines. My mother used to tell me that the pebbles were as they were because the sea had once been there. As I have said, at heart she remained a countrywoman all her life, and many things kept their mystery for her. Awe was in her voice as she spoke of the sea once having covered those hills, and I felt it as I listened though I did not know the word.

It was here that my mother taught me about the difference between ordinary heather, which there was a lot of, though an unusually pale, mauvish-blue colour which I am not sure I should like if I saw it today, and 'bell-heather', which comes in the flower-books as fine-leaved heath, and is a bright sharp purple. It was much rarer. Very occasionally we found cross-leaved heath as well: but my mother did not know this was a third kind.

I used also to collect the fir-cones. So did my mother, but for something else. Each afternoon when we went home the shopping basket would be full of fir-cones. They replaced the dinner; and sometimes a piece or so of dead wood would be fitted into my push-chair as well, or I would hold it as we wheeled along. But when my mother took a good-sized piece of wood she cleared off quickly, though with a touch of something fiercely defiant. Fir-cones and pieces of dead wood were so different for her, because she had some idea, though perhaps a confused one, of the rural privilege of taking fuel from woods: you might but then again you mightn't, she knew that. Anything like country thievery filled her with a poacher's, a gipsy's mixed feelings of fear, delight, desperate courage, and urge to grab and flee. Why she had these primitive reactions I don't quite know: perhaps her childhood mentality had been partly formed by that of the servant they had—children were often nearer to servants than to their parents. Partly, some of her cousins on her mother's side (though her mother was such a snob) were splendid country lads, boisterous and devil-may-care, and in their youth got up to all sorts of country mischief. Partly, for a long time in the English countryside it has really been war between the landed and the landless, and my mother thought like the landless.

Anyhow, my mother was building up a little scrap of a fuel-hoard against the winter. And winter was coming, for in the last week or so of our excursions to Shirley, before I went back to school, we could feel the cold tang in the air in the mornings, and sometimes in the afternoons as we came home and the blue mist began to form, and my mother began to worry that I might not be warm enough. It was true that she kept warm striding along, while my feet got cold as I had to sit still. But then, she had to do the work.

Cold was an important thing in the lives of children, and adults too, in those days. I remember my surprise the first time I woke up to see the leaf patterns that the frost had made on our bedroom windows, and also the surprise of finding only a dull grey light, more like a half dark, in the veranda, because the glass roof was covered with snow. It seemed strange that snow could be so white, but make the light so grey. We used to push the snow off with a broom that we held at arm's length through the back bedroom window. It fell with a swishy plop. When I was six or seven there was a severe winter, and once or twice, first thing in the morning, there were icicles hanging from the brass kitchen tap that brought us our cold water. There was only this one tap in the whole system, by the way; so when the washer needed changing, my father had to do it in the full force of the water, that ripped in hard white spurts out of the pipe, with a harsh swishing noise, almost a roar, as it came, and jetted and fountained up in the air, and all over him, as he put the faucet back. If he had to mend the tap in the very cold weather he got very angry. So we used to leave it for a long time in winter, and you could listen to the tinkle of the drips into the bowl, getting slowly faster as the days went by and the washer wore away.

The lavatory was outside the back door, through another door off the veranda, and this made it fresh and secluded. But several times in winter the cistern froze. I can remember my father once trying—with success—to thaw the pipe with a candle-flame. We used sometimes to burn a small oil lamp in the lavatory. It burnt very bright yellow, down there on the floor.

When you are a child, a good deal of cold is a stimulus and an excitement: then there comes a point, either with cold and wind, or with a deep still cold, when you begin to be afraid: you have a dim sense that experience ranges out to much greater extremes than anything you know. Once I went up alone, in the dark and the frost, on the top of a bus—most buses had open tops then. It was excitingly cold waiting for it to start; but once it was going fast, and swaying a lot as they always seemed to, the cold became sharp in quite a new way, even though I held over me the canvas cover the upstairs seats had in those days. I had to wait until the first stop before I could come down the open stairs, and I got frozen and very frightened. Another surprise about cold was first seeing blizzard weather while waiting for a bus by my school at the top of South Norwood Hill. My mother and I watched the gusts of snow swirling and driving through the big chestnut trees in the churchyard. A third surprise, though not a painful one, was how snow went brown when it thawed: and it went all the browner, because of all the gravel they threw on the roads. There were big grey metal boxes in the street, that were kept stocked up with gravel for frosty weather. This gravel was to help the horses, so it was very special and out of bounds: only the very bad boys clutched it in handfuls and threw it at each other. The roadmen swished it noisily, in big arcs, across the road with their shovels.

Although I can remember the pain of being very cold indeed, so that my ears and nose and toes and fingers used to feel a kind of cutting burning numbness, (and it hurt even more when you got warm again), I didn't want for warm clothes, and we had fires at home. Being cold in this way was simply a part of how one lived. There were long walks to do, and long waits for buses. Sometimes the buses ran very late—especially in the brown London fogs. In the end, two or three or four might arrive together—once I saw seven in a row—and of course the more it was foggy or frosty the more likely it was that this would happen. There were no bus shelters. People stamping and stomping disconsolately up and down, or hunched into their coats, were a familiar sight at bus-stops. Looking back, this seems especially so after dark: I think the evening buses were often very infrequent, and certainly they were often nearly empty when at last they did come.

My mother used to get very cold indeed, because most of her gloves were thin ones—once she had a pair of big gloves that were leather inside and wonderfully, lovably soft dark fur outside; but these were no good for her, the palms were as thin as paper. Also, if it was rainy or snowy, the wet came through her shoes. She had bad chilblains every winter, and her hands used to chap.

My father was very resistant to cold; and he needed to be. The time came when he bought himself a pair of oilskin cycle leggings, but before that he came in from his ride home soaked up to the groin when the roads were running with the rain. Quite often he would be unable to speak, for ten minutes or a quarter of an hour, when he came in out of the frost. He would pull a chair close to the fire, and lean forward towards it, and after a while stretch his hands—which remained surprisingly shapely, for all the work they did—out in front of it. He used to unbend his fingers slowly. My mother admired him for these journeys.

I myself was kept warmer than my parents because I used to have fingerless gloves of close thick cloth, and later what we called 'astrakhan' gloves—the outer side made of dark brown wool woven to a close crinkly surface; not of course the real thing, but I was well looked after. Also, when I first went to school and for about two years after that, I had brown gaiters that went from my shoes to over my knees. They did up with a lace that went over studs and drew the two edges together, and buttoned at the top, and kept my legs very warm indeed. I also had sound brown boots. My, I was looked after.

We rarely lacked fuel and if we did it was usually just because we were waiting for it to come. I recall one time when my mother and father talked over what they could find to burn —something to break up, I mean, like a bit of the chicken shed —but I no longer know if that was simply because the coal had not come, or because we were short of money to order it. There was another time when we were cold enough to notice with interest that a little heat came from the gas-mantle. The bedroom was fiendishly cold, but we had a big stone hot-water-bottle, which my mother used to make woollen covers for—they wore out from time to time—and which we shared round. Later we had two. I used always to undress in front of the living-room fire in cold weather and then make a rush for bed; and I think my father did the same, but not my mother. When I was small she used to wrap me in a blanket and carry me up the stairs. All the same I must have got cold, because I can remember how long I used to spend putting my feet on the stone bottle all the ways I could find, trying to get my feet warm. To warm the tops of one's feet on a stone hot-water-bottle is quite a difficult thing. Sometimes my mother would come and rub my feet or my legs for me, if I couldn't get warm. Since then I have done it for my own children. We used to put our overcoats on the beds in cold weather, and sometimes our clothes as well; but we didn't know how to do this so that our underclothes would be warm in the morning from our sleeping bodies; and getting up and putting on ice-cold clothes in a cold bedroom used to be a bad moment. It was also a bad moment to empty one's bowels in the morning in the veranda lavatory. We always used chamber-pots if we wanted to make water during the night.

Because our front room was let, and we only lit the copper in the kitchen for the washing or to make hot water to ladle out into the bath, there was really only one fire to think about: the kitchen range in the living-room. My mother sometimes used the oven for roasting, and sometimes cooked in saucepans on the top. Usually she had a kettle boiling on it, or simmering on the hob. This fire burnt well, but it was small, and there was no question of burning wood on it. So we depended on the coal-man. It was an exciting moment when the coal came, the sacks stacked on a big heavy dray that had a low iron rail at the sides and back, and a high bow-shaped, ornamental rail at the front, with the merchant's name painted on a fine bow-shaped plate. It was this high front rail that the sacks were stacked against: sometimes they would be two sacks high at the front. The drays would be pulled by two big horses, dark brown usually, with black manes that were left long, and flowing fetlocks of a dirty white. The colliers wasted no time. In their blackened overalls and grimy leather hoods, one would thunder on the door, and the very moment it was opened the other would be stomping in with the first sack. To reach the coal-hole they had to march down the front hall, and through the living-room. They ought to have gone straight forward, through the glass doors in the kitchen; but usually they had to turn left and go out to the veranda through the scullery instead. Their heavy boots clattered and boomed on the floor. Their leather hoods came right down their backs. Their faces and hands were an odd silvery-black, which is coal and sweat mixed. They always hurried. If my toys were on the floor when the coal came, I had to sweep them aside at top speed. The colliers disappeared out the back, and then came the roar of the coal as they poured it through. When they had done, they left at once, abruptly, heavily. Often I used to see the coal carts in the street, the collier standing up to drive his horses, waving his long whip. Sometimes they made them canter. With very full loads, or if they were going up the really steep slopes like the one by the Portland Road railway bridge, they had three or even four horses, but I never saw them canter with more than two.

# Chapter four

# Some shops and some callers

The centre of South Norwood was really the cross-roads where South Norwood Hill, crossing the High Street, turned into Portland Road. Just above the cross-roads, on the right, was the Stanley Technical School, an ornate but (as I realized when I saw it years later) quite unusually ugly building. Ugliness like that is a real achievement, it has its own perverse distinction. Nevertheless, the Stanley School was at once the most ambitious piece of architecture, and the loftiest educational establishment, which I then knew. Opposite was the Fire Station. One of the firemen had a son who went to my school, and when I was six or seven I went to a Christmas party in a flat over the engines—an enormous party, maybe forty children, and lots of grown-ups idling about with their hands folded, waiting for a chance to tick us off. As for the fire-engines, I can only say that brass does not shine now as it did then. There must have been a change in the metal. The big bonnets of those two engines glittered so much that they could hurt your eyes.

35

Round the corner was Gale's the drapers, the biggest shop we ever went to, unless we went for a day to Croydon. I believe that Gale's even had two floors. Its chief wonder for me was the network of cash-railways that ran everywhere through it. When you bought something, the assistant wrote out a bill, wrapped your money in it, and put the whole thing into a metal capsule which she unscrewed from a long wire on a bracket overhead. Then she screwed it back on to its base (which had a wheel on the top, mounted on the wire) and pulled down a handle on a long string. She let it go, that released the spring, a bell tinged loudly, and capsule and wheel were shot off and rolled swiftly along the wire making a noise like a tram, only quiet not loud. And it swayed from side to side like a tram too. Sometimes it even had to switch its way round a corner before it arrived at the cash-desk. There, all day long, sat an extraordinarily privileged woman. She waited for the little chariots to arrive, unwrapped the screws of paper in them, loaded them up again with change, and fired them off back along the wires in all directions. That was the job to have . . .

Along the High Street, only just beyond Gale's but on the other side, was a small florist's called 'Quelque Fleurs'. Mrs. Figg, one of our neighbours, was very proud when her daughter got a job there. She said the name so that it ran almost like 'manicure'; and obliged my mother with the information that it meant a 'basket of flowers'. My mother said it the same way, but knew its real meaning: so that was another one against Mrs. Figg—not that my mother put her right, and not that she could have done because you couldn't get a word in edgeways with Mrs. Figg, as I shall say later. That was also pretty near the frontier of my mother's knowledge of French.

Portland Road begins with a quite steep slope downhill, to get under the railway bridge. In those days the road was paved with granite blocks. The horses had a shoe on the wheel more or less all the way down South Norwood Hill, but on this bit they sometimes had two shoes on. Even so, the dray-horses, with heavy loads of coal or sacks of meal, had to thrust hard back against the traces. They crinkled their lips open loosely, and they looked wild and you saw the scared whites of their eyes. Their big muscles and tendons were straining, their loose thick fetlocks were flopping, as they sought a foothold on the granite blocks polished blue with wear. In the dark, their iron hooves struck sparks.

Under the bridge was where Jumbo sold his newspapers from a wooden box. He was a short, thick-set man; not a dwarf but not a normal man either. He never washed, so his face was dark brown, and he had a great rough beard. His clothes must have been given him: they were all a lot too big. In cold weather he wrapped himself in newspapers—he made a newspaper cloak over his shoulders, and a big skirt which he kept in at his waist with a piece of string. He always sold the *Evening Standard*; but he couldn't say that right, or anything else either. 'Dun-dud', he used to say: 'Dun-dud'. He hobbled as he walked, a sheaf of papers under each arm. I think this 'Dun-dud' was where the name *Jumbo* came from. No one knew any other name for him. When he'd done enough paper-selling, he used to put his box over the iron fence on the rail-way embankment, and stomp and limp off down lower Albert Road. I think he slept on the sewage farm: he may have found a warm corner near the incinerator.

Besides Jumbo, there was a real dwarf. He too was a heavy-built man (except the legs), with big dark eyes that shone, and a black beard. It had ripples in it and looked silky. I saw him walking about but I didn't ever see him doing anything—not work, I mean, like selling papers. And there was also one negro man, a very thin one. He seemed always to be in his overcoat, grey herring-bone, his hands down in the pockets and a trilby hat with a very narrow brim on top of his sad face. My, his arms and legs were long. I never saw him with anyone. Before long, of course, I understood how he was a different kind of thing from Jumbo or the dwarf; but you had

**37**

to learn that, because there was only one of him, the way there was only one of them.

At the first corner in Portland Road, beyond the railway bridge, was the big seed and meal store, with maize and meal for chickens, and a dozen other such things, ranged along the front of the counter in hessian sacks with the necks rolled down. When my mother and father were buying, I used to put my hand into each sack, and let the stuff in it trickle back through my fingers. Maize makes a light whispering rattle; bone-meal is a dry dust that leaves your fingers powdery. All the smells were soft and clean-seeming. The man's brown drill overall was clean—crisp too, washed many times, and very much ironed.

Lower down on the other side was our only fish-shop save for one right away in the High Street. My father was specially fond of fish, perhaps through living so near the sea as a boy; and we loved shell-fish too, and used to buy shrimps for a treat—by the half-pint they were sold, and much cheaper in proportion than they are now. The shop was run by a man with his son and two daughters; and the whole family had deformed hands, just a thumb and one finger. At first I thought they had hurt themselves cutting up the fish. Little by little I noticed they all had the same thing wrong, and my mother said it ran in the family. The old woman was there sometimes. Her hands were all right.

Further down the road, back on the other side, was the Central Cinema, where at one time we used all three to go every Wednesday after tea. They were silent films in those days, with actors and actresses like Rudolph Valentino and the ex-heavyweight boxer Gene Tunney ('Jeannie' we used to say it), Mary Pickford, Myrna Loy and Boris Karloff. There was also a Western serial each week, with the train and the buggy converging at the level crossing as the final minutes ran out, or Tom Mix dropping right on top of the bandit's waggon. He sailed through the air by climbing up a fir-tree and then swinging down as he made it bend over in a great drooping arch. Also there was Buck Jones with his sheriff's star. Thanks to the camera-man, he never missed a shot.

Music was supplied by two ladies in black frocks. Each of them thundered at a grand piano. They faced and smiled at each other across the front of the auditorium, and sometimes, in unison, they smiled at the audience. Each one of them wore a crimson rose on her bosom. They could neither of them play as well as my mother, but they could play very loud. When the cinema was over, we always did the same thing; we bought fish and chips at a shop opposite, and walked home down Harrington Road eating the food and re-living the film. Those walks home were among the happiest or at least the gayest moments of my whole childhood. After the cinema the daylight used to seem very white and bright, and I would be dazzled at first; but the naive magic of the film world spread over into it. At this time—it was different after I was nine, when my life greatly changed—I had no scope for playing Tom Mix; but I had a fine silver six-shooter and played Buck Jones a lot. Once, when I was ill in bed, and portly Dr. Smith put his big moustache round the door to come and see me, I gave him a quick-on-the-draw hands-up with my six-shooter. He was not amused. He was a sour or at least a gruff man; but a good doctor. Mr. Bevis the dentist, by the way, also lived down Selhurst Road in one of the big houses on the way to Croydon; but he was quite different. He seemed quite the most superior man I knew, and spoke very little, slowly, in a quiet refined voice. He had extraordinarily clean hands with cool fingers, and very shiny boots: he wore boots because one leg had been amputated at the hip during the war. Now he had a cork one; you couldn't tell except that that leg didn't bend at the knee, and he walked slowly. His other relic from the war, besides his cork leg, was a black military moustache, clipped very short.

It was in Harrington Road, that we walked along so gleefully with our fish and chips, that I lost Jack. Jack was a big black-and-tan retriever dog which we found outside our front door one day, and he wouldn't go away. So we kept him, and I got very fond of him. I don't remember, but we either didn't report finding him to the Police Station, or if we did he wasn't claimed. We had Jack a good six months, and that was fine. He was a big clever dog, with a nice clean smell. Then one day my mother and I were walking in Harrington Road, with Jack too, and suddenly he took to his heels, raced off up the street, and pranced and danced all over a tall dark man in a grey trilby and navy blue overcoat. The man burst into roars of joy, and they pranced and danced about together for a minute in great spirits. So Jack had found his master, not the other way round, and he didn't call him Jack at all—that was just our name—but 'Monday' or something like that. It was no good to argue, because even if the man had been in two minds about taking him away, Jack (Monday), was not in two minds. He'd found the real thing again, and there was no question of trying to keep him; so we let the two of them go off, larking and leaping about down the street and out of sight.

Our shops were in Harrington Road, at the junction with Albert Road, where the 'Albert' itself was: I used to see the children hanging about outside, but never had to myself. (When my mother went into the 'Signal' to buy Mrs. Pie's quart—I'll explain about that later—she used to make me stand by the lamp-post, right away from the pub door.) There was a butcher, who was a black-eyed fierce-moustached man in a grey cap always, and blue-and-white striped butcher's apron, and a black leather thumbstall over his left thumb, which he'd mutilated—I never saw how—with chopping at the meat. In Rogers's the grocer's, they had more sacks of meal and corn, and big tin canisters, black, with faded gold characters on them, for the tea and rice and the rest. Mr. Rogers had a collection of big knives, the blades long, the handles black; and also a bacon-slicing machine. He had a short-bladed knife, broad but shaped down to a point, to snick out the bone with, and then he put the bacon-joint under the shiny metal teeth on the machine, and the crisp, swishing, sound of slicing

40

the rashers would begin. He cut his cheese with a wire. It was a black wire: I wonder if he ever cleaned it? His cheddar was a deep yellow, like butter, and he sold gorgonzola, which was cheap in those days and which all three of us delighted in.

I used to go shopping alone to Rogers. Once a big boy strolled along with me, got into talk, and seemed a very fine superior boy. Next he offered to carry my basket—I was five—and next he offered to carry my shilling. When I said no, he demanded to carry the shilling or he'd throw the basket over the wall—by now we were walking beside the garden wall of Mr. Rogers himself. But of course, when in much trouble of mind I gave him the shilling, he ran off at once and threw the basket over the wall into the bargain. Mr. Rogers, and Miss Rogers, and my mother too, were very nice to me; but really I was lucky to have this happen so young, and no worse—I learnt a lot from it. As for that boy, I heard about him later. He got into bad ways; further in I mean.

Going back home the other way, along Harrington Road, there were two more shops. One was a little grocer's shop kept by a bad-tempered elderly man. I forget his name but I remember his cap and white moustache and how he seemed unfriendly. He had a dingy little shop with very little stock, but we used to buy brown sugar from him sometimes, because it was a farthing a pound cheaper. It was in an alley behind this shop that, on my seventh birthday, I got a black eye—not in a fight but from a surprise attack. After it the other boy disappeared; but he needn't have, I could tell from how he blacked the one eye that he could have blacked the other too. My mother was very ill at the time, and afterwards often reproached me with how I went home and stood at the foot of the bed for her to have to look at, with my eye purple and closing fast.

The other shop was Mr. Blackman's. This was the shop for sweets, cigarettes and papers. I used often to go here alone, because it was the nearest shop to my house. I bought packets of 'Weights' for my father (who smoked 50 or 60 of these a

day, and in the end died of fibrositis of the lungs—so-called);
or Player's Medium, with the two different-sized lighthouses
and the bearded sailor he liked so much, or Wills's Gold Flake,
if he felt better off. Wills's 'Woodbines' were the same price
as Player's 'Weights' (ten for fourpence) but my father thought
them a low cigarette. He would have been giving up if he'd
gone over to Woodbines. I don't know why this was. At
Blackman's I could buy sherbet fountains for a halfpenny,
or loose sherbet which was cheaper still, and we sometimes
made a drink with it. But then you missed the special taste of
licking the sherbet off the yellow paper and the cheap cardboard of the fountain. Ha'penny hardsticks were the other
thing I specially liked; this very hard liquorice, really too hard
until you are six or seven, lasted a great time, and eating it in
the end gave me a sense of achievement as well as a nice taste.
I also had comics from this shop: *Tiger Tim's Weekly* at
first—and I had a 'sailor suit' (much liked by devoted parents
for their children in those far-off days) with *H.M.S. Tiger*
round the hat. Later I had *The Skipper* or *The Modern
Boy*. Charlie Crabb up the road had *The Rainbow* and
later *The Magnet*: so I left these alone, a little I think in the
spirit that my father left Woodbines alone. When I was eight
I was a fluent reader, and I bought several fourpenny paper-
bound books about highwaymen. These, and pirates, were
then almost the staple imaginative diet for boys placed as I
was. Black Bess and the ride to York took on extra meaning
for me because of how my mother had brought me up to see
animals as important.

I used also to go round to Blackman's for cakes. Swiss rolls
and so-called French cream sponges were our chief treats: the
latter had artificial cream and jam together in them, and seemed
fine. I now find them dreadful. There were also chocolate rolls
with another kind of cream, almost like sweet creamy cheese.
These had a taste that left something to be desired, but they
seemed rather grown-up eating, and I used to make an
effort.

To an adult these shops were all very close (though a child would find the distance greater). But even so, much of our food came to the door. The milkman, in a uniform cap and a blue-and-white apron, wheeled his milk-trolley with a big brass churn on it. 'Mi-ook O!' he used to cry. His three measures, made of zinc, and very scoured, hung over a metal bar by the handle of his trolley, and he filled them from the tap of the churn and poured the bubbly milk into our jug. In the house we kept flies out of the milk by a square of gauze over the top of the jug; it stayed in place because it was weighted with a big round bead at each corner. There was a greengrocer's shop in Harrington Road, but greengroceries also came to the door on a big wooden trolley with a sloping top; the sort you could make into a little stall by fixing a bit of awning over it. In the afternoon the muffin man sometimes came, with his stately tread, and a big hand-bell he clanged as he marched along. His tray of muffins he carried on his head without holding it— under the tray was a woollen ring, knitted in dark blue and stuffed like a cushion.

Other people called in the way of business too. The gas-man used to come right inside, swiftly and quietly, and make a dive for the gas-meter under the stairs to empty out the shillings. Once or twice, in needy times, my mother or my father had taken the thin, supple-bladed knife we had for the cooking to the slot of that meter: but they never had any luck, if that is the word.

Besides the gas-man who came to the house, I used to see the lamp-lighter. He rode round on his bicycle at dusk, with a long pole, shiny brown, over his shoulder. It had a brass end, which he used to push up through a hole in the base of the lamp, and that turned on the main jet. What lit it was the tiny flame of the pilot jet, that you could see all day, burning blue, if you had a good look. In midwinter you saw the lamp-lighter in the mornings, putting his lamps out.

The old-iron man used to come down the street too, calling 'any-old iron?' to the tune of:

as he rattled the reins of his little cart the small skinny brown horse pulled. But we never had any.

Another cart, with another little brown horse, also came from time to time, with the driver calling 'rag-a-bo-one!' to the same tune but deeper and slower. Miss Chapman once had one of her chairs re-caned by the man who called for that, and sat on the granite kerb to do it. The knife-grinder man also had a street cry, and I liked him the best. When he got a job he let a frame down on his bicycle; then he could use the pedals to drive the carborundum wheel mounted above the handlebars. The knife made a harsh, sizzling noise, almost fierce, as it came down on the dark grey wheel, and shot the sparks up in a thick abrupt spurt. But mostly we sharpened our knives, or at least the carving knife, on the back step, to and fro, squitch-squetch, squitch-squetch—it doesn't make the same noise both ways, but I can't say why not.

When the sweep came, his face would be blacker than the coalman's, and his eyes very white. He would get down on his knees at the kitchen range; and after watching one or two of his rods go up the chimney, I would run out into the garden, to see his black brush twirl merrily out of the chimney-top, then go down again. Just once or twice we saw a sweep's brush come up from other people's chimneys. It was always a gay sight for some reason. Many people had chimney-cowls to make the draught right. These used to go round in the wind, sometimes slowly, sometimes fast, and were fun to watch: but I never saw a sweep's brush come out of a cowl. I suppose they can't.

On Mondays the rent-collector came for the week's rent: often enough it was ready for him on the mantelpiece, but occasionally we thought it best to go out all day on Monday.

That did for him; but the next Monday would be that much worse.

Then there were hawkers. I knew from the kitchen when my mother opened the door to a hawker, because of the sudden flood of confident ingratiation, more or less refined, that burst through the house. Sometimes they were selling ribbons or combs or brushes, but often it turned soon enough into a hard-luck story. When they combined a la-di-da voice with their foot in the door, my mother would get annoyed. 'Smarmy fellow!' she would say after she had got rid of them, stressing it as if the second word meant a lot as well as the first. But often these random callers were of another kind: middle-aged or elderly men, their old clothes carefully brushed up, who called to ask if by any chance we had a coat, or a scarf, or a pair of shoes or gloves, that we didn't happen to want, as they happened to need this badly because of their health, or to get a 'post', or whatever it was. Some of these men were educated people, and not very like the hawkers who 'put it on' (as we said). My mother used to talk long with one or two of them, and try to help them; and the two would stand at the door and exchange reflections and maxims about life and the conduct of life; a kind of folk-philosophy, stoical yet sentimental, always much the same because it always does the same job. All this was in the Hard '20s, of course.

In those days there were quite often men who sang in the street, even in our quiet suburban back-street. They used to walk slowly up the middle, with their hats in their hands, singing with great zeal and expression. One sang '*O sole mio!*' in a very Italian style. This was a song which my father, who had a pleasant tenor voice, used to begin sometimes in English —'Oh what a nice thing, Is a summer's day-ay . . . and all the little birds be-Gin To Sing'. But he didn't know all the words. I used to be sent out with a penny to run and give to the street-singer. Sometimes their faces lit up, but often they were deep in song, they hardly noticed. If you got a competence, and liked your own voice, it was perhaps no bad thing to be a street-singer in those days. Today, one would hardly fit into the scheme of things; but then it was a very normal thing to be. Once or twice we had the three-man band, often to be seen in Portland Road, come up our street: a soulful cornet, a bass-drum, and a piccolo I think there was. They also went up the middle of the street. Sometimes you would hear them walking quite a long way with just the big drum plonking. This built up the suspense. Often, too, the organ-grinder came along. I was intrigued by how his music always seemed to begin in the middle of a tune, and very loud; and when my mother pointed out to me that the speed he turned the handle had nothing to do with the speed of the music, I was intrigued by that too, and used to watch his arm a long while.

One brass-instrument player lived in our street. This was Mr. Beckford, who lived in the house next to Charlie Crabb's house. I forget what he did for a living—he was a respectable man with a steady job of some kind—but he played the euphonium in the Salvation Army band which floated its massed silver notes into the air every weekend in Portland Road, and sometimes at the top of our road or just round the corner. I often saw him going off or coming home, his euphonium under his arm and his feet coming out half-sideways from under his deep blue Salvation Army frock-coat. ('Walking with your feet at a quarter to one' my mother called this.) But he was a fierce, self-righteous, stand-offish man, and he wouldn't unbend my way at all. He certainly had fierce moustaches, in two great bushy waves across his face. Once, just as he was going into his front door, I called out after him, as bad boys often did then in the streets. 'Old Whiskery Beckford', I cried: which in fact was what I'd heard my parents call him. Then I ran off home and got inside. But sure enough, in a minute or so he was beating a tattoo at our knocker. 'Do you know what your boy called me?', he demanded irately of my mother '—Old Whiskery Beckford!' But she saw at once where the phrase had come from, and was only just able to apologize ('coming the duchess', as we called it, as much as she could) and get the door shut, before she had a fit of the giggles with me in the hall.

Sometimes we had people call at the house in the name of religion. Those who simply came to give us Bibles or Testaments and to explain what Christianity was had no luck. My mother was after all a church organist's daughter, she had sung in the choir, she was not going to be treated like a heathen. She had a Bible, which was full of mementos and pressed flowers (it still is), and which she sometimes read in; just as she liked the stoical parts of the Prayer-Book (in the baptismal or burial service) and sometimes sang verses of the psalms to herself because she was proud she could do the pointing. The straight evangelists got nowhere with her. But a Christadelphian who called when I was seven or eight got on much better. He came several times, gave her a book, inexpensively bound in blue and gold, which she studied with deep attention, and also had a talk or so with my father: who was interested too, though rather bewildered.

The Christadelphian had such a success, for the very reason that what he offered was something very primitive. Many years later, when I had become a teacher of English, and studied the Ptolemaic astronomy because it turned up in Chaucer or Milton, I found to my surprise that I was familiar, from long ago, with its main features. They had formed the basis of the Christadelphian's book, along with the Ptolemaic hieroglyphs for the heavenly bodies, the twelve signs of the zodiac, and all the rest of the rigmarole. There were also a few vestigial traces of alchemy—fire, and I think also mercury, had potencies which in no way followed from how we actually had knowledge of them, and met them in the grate or thermometer. With this went a little number-mysticism, and above all, a vivid if vague millennium-mumbo-jumbo, which explained, at the same time as it was allegedly confirmed by, prophecies in the Book of Daniel and the Revelation of Saint John the Divine.

My mother and particularly my father were both genuinely

superstitious. Once or twice a crow came and cawed on the roof-tops. That was very bad. My father had a horror of the number thirteen, and ladders in the street; and was in deep misery for a whole day or so, when I was about six, because my mother accidentally broke a mirror. This upset her too. Throughout all these years she never failed to throw spilt salt over her left shoulder. Black cats, though, and picking up pins, were good. But her deepest superstitions were all religious. I put it this way on purpose: what drew her, what kindled her imagination, was what the sophisticated on either side would agree to call the more superstitious part of religion; and I recount this fact because I believe that in this she was widely representative of ordinary people over millennia. The creative-redemptive side of Christianity aroused neither her imagination nor her credence. She knew Salvation Army songs like:

> Throw out the life-line!
> Throw out the life-line—
> Someone is sinking to-da-ay!

But what she did was sing the rude words instead.

To be sure, she didn't believe the other side enough to make her go to church or pray (save very rarely and at some disastrously bad time: though she carefully taught me to pray, and for several years it was a long-drawn-out fetish with me, every night of my life). But what could really take possession of her mind, striking at her through fear and awe, was the thought of Hell and Satan, and the idea of 'the End of the World'. Her eschatology was primitive but sensible and consistent. On the whole, she sensed that there was no after-life; but in so far as there might be one, her idea of it was not sophisticated or diluted. She found no difficulty in believing that music would be enough for the saints; but on the other hand, expressions like 'hell-fire' and 'Lucifer, son of the morning' had fixed themselves deeply and simply in her mind. She would have responded quickly and warmly to a certain kind of sophisticated comment on these ideas (such as that the phrase about Lucifer referred not to Satan at all, but one of the planets); but they hadn't come her way.

The cozifying dilutions of modern Christianity would simply, I am glad to say, have bored her. Satan and Hell were uncertain enough to be discountable risks for her; but if they did indeed exist, the former was much more personal than God, and likely (God, in our sector of creation, being self-evidently half-hearted or incompetent) to be much the nearer. Hell was simply where you were likely to go when you died, though it was more likely that you went nowhere save into the ground. If it did exist, it had no trees but plenty of fires, and we fully believed that the truly wicked lived in these in eternal torment. But in our tradition some vestigial trace of Limbo survived; and we all three filtered it, as it were, right through Hell. So we thought that in these interstices, harmless but godless people like ourselves could hope to be left alone.

An apocalyptic tradition was quite strong in my family, though in fragments, one could say, and divorced from its wider meanings. 'Till doomsday' was a common idiom in those days (it seems to have gone now). 'The last trump', and 'the crack of doom' were phrases my mother knew, she scarcely knew from where; and 'Armageddon' was an idea that had been made familiar by politicians and the press in the context of the First World War. Other ideas from the Apocalypse were also, vaguely, among the folk-lore of our part of the population: the Scarlet Woman, the Mark of the Beast, the Number of the Beast. These were all things you could turn over in your mind and think about; and since we did not live in a society which challenged us with awkward questions, until we had to assume a critical attitude towards our mythology, they were not immediately different for us from the ascent of Elijah, the Trojans, the wicked Richard III, Bluebeard, Dr. Crippen, or the Kaiser.

Anyone who supposes that I am reading into the mentality of my parents the lack of logic and of categorization that

**49**

belonged in fact only to the world of a child, should consider
one fact which is enough by itself to disprove that. There was
much interest in Ancient Egypt among ordinary people in
these years, due in large part to the discovery of the tomb of
Tutenkhamon (1922). of which the popular press made a great
thing. But at much the same time, F. W. Chapman published
his work on the number-mysteries of the Great Pyramids. I forget when these predicted the End of the World, but it was at
some time which is now in the fairly remote past. Assuming
always that the world has not yet ended (which some may doubt),
the whole subject was strictly comparable with the apocalyptics
of our Christadelphian. But it was discussed and explained in
articles that went on for page after page in the popular daily
newspapers. Millions of English people, if they did not actually
believe these ideas about the pyramid measurements and the
predictions which were derived from them, at any rate found
them interesting, thought-provoking, perhaps emotionally dis-
turbing. I remember that my father did, and I think that it was
by drawing on this that the Christadelphian drew him into the
talk.

The fact is, that for ordinary people at that time, the whole
idea of Apocalypse in a curious way made sense of their experience, and gave it an order which otherwise it lacked. In the
main, their world was one of hard work for slight or chancy
rewards, of near want or unearned misfortune far more often
than its opposite, and of extreme but meaningless inequality.
Occasionally, on the other hand, something in their life gave
them the idea of a fulness and order which mostly they lacked.
It struck all the sharper for being so rare and so different. For
inadequacy and disorder, truly enough the staple of their life,
to grow to a head, become cataclysmic, destroy itself in world-
wide disaster, and be replaced by its own opposite (an opposite
which they knew to exist now, but in subordination as it were)
—this made sense of their experience, and perhaps made it
seem more rewarding. More sophisticated people have another
image of life, because war, unemployment, illness, are things

(even when they strike personally) which they can see as part of a system and understand from what they know of history, social science, social medicine, and the laws of probability. And today, moreover, the plainest of plain men lives in a world where life is full of at least the offer of rewards, not hardships; and where the general image of society is that it is rationally and systematically ordered so as to give people what they want. These notions are profoundly, transformingly novel, at least for plain men. In my childhood, there was little enough feeling even that people ought to have what they wanted; and there was no feeling that society was ordered so as to give it them. You just clutched in the sea.

Hence the strength of a vague Stoicism; and millennium-mumbo-jumbo was a kind of counterpart. This is why I used to see the Christadelphian coming along by the big may tree at the end of our road (he always came the same way, from down the hill) and know that my mother would talk to him long and earnestly. He brought to our little road a message deeply dubious, but deeply interesting too; and when, passing St. Mark's Church, we saw the bible placard which read 'Repent: for the Kingdom of God is at Hand', that only showed that it might be the Christadelphian who saw clearly—he alone—what others saw dimly, or put up on a board and then forgot.

# Chapter five

# We too could polish flints

What—limited as we admittedly were—could we do? What did we know? What, perhaps one could ask, was our culture? By this I do not mean intellectual culture as I was later to know it, because of that we had none. During my childhood, my mother read and re-read Alexandre Dumas' *The Three Musketeers* and *Twenty Years After*, and Hardy's *Tess of the d'Urbervilles*. She identified herself a little with Tess, and rightly: not because of Tess's amorous misfortunes, but because these were merely what helped to drive Tess from a secure niche in a rural society. In a way this had happened to my mother also; though it had taken place already, in part, with *her* mother, and this she did not understand.

Besides these three novels, she had an anthology of poetry and prose, which was called *The Open Road*. It had illustrated end-papers, one of an empty country road in sunlight, and the other of one under the moon. These made a deep impression on me. I came across a copy of this book, quite by chance, in my mid-forties, and when the first end-paper opened for me,

52

it was a moment of sudden heightened awareness such as even the return of things treasured in the past can seldom bring. In this book there were one or two poems by William Barnes that my mother read aloud or quoted with affection, partly because of the West-Country dialect which was not far from her own.

Otherwise we had no contact with 'literature'. We had a copy of W. J. Locke's *Joyous Adventures of Aristide Pujol*— my mother pronounced the christian name of this jaunty, sentimental, life-loving little commercial traveller so as to rhyme with 'not only Mrs. but *Mr.* D'; *The Blue Lagoon* (I forget the author); Margaret Kennedy's *The Constant Nymph*; Warwick Deeping's *Sorrell & Son*; and Sheila Kaye-Smith's *The Rose and the Crown*. These were all much-loved books: the last especially, because once again of its West-Country dialect. Besides these, we had some knowledge of characters in Dickens—Scrooge; Mr. Pickwick (who was illustrated on a fancy biscuit-tin which stood on our mantel-shelf for years: but I remember that we couldn't place all the four Dickens characters on that tin, one on each side); and I think Squeers, and Oliver Twist asking for more. Scrooge and Pickwick were known to us as characters, but these last two we knew merely for isolated incidents that they came in. They really belonged to the family's stock of stories or indeed legends. In one way it would be reasonable to put them along with the Bible stories we knew: the Garden of Eden, crossing the Red Sea, Jonah, David playing the harp for Saul, Joshua's trumpet and the walls of Jericho (my mother was always drawn to anything musical), Abraham, Isaac and the ram (so she was to anything about parental love), the burning bush, the Flood (especially the raven and doves episode), and the Lord calling to Samuel in the night. This last crossed in my mother's mind with the young Handel's being found at night playing the organ.

Then there was Daniel in the lion's den, Shadrach and the rest in the fiery furnace, and Sodom and Gomorrah. The pillar of salt struck me a lot; but I still don't know for sure what they did in Gomorrah. My mother sometimes read in the Old Testament, but it was a central book for her only in that it was the store-house of so many of the tales that made up her culture. The ways of the Creator, the history of his Chosen People, were not how she saw its contents. From the New Testament we had the Nativity and Crucifixion (thanks in part to Stainer) and one or two other things; but what had most caught my mother's imagination was the thumb-mark of Christ which you can see on the haddock-fish. She showed me this quite seriously, and she would have felt unhappy indeed if someone had forced her to give the idea up—more so than she would have done denying the Trinity or Incarnation probably. Christianity was genuinely a felt mythology for her, though barely religious in the stricter, the theological sense.

We also had some songs and rhymes at our command. My father knew:

> Tomorrow is my wedding-day:
> Ten thousand pounds I'll give away! (*cheers*)
> . . . On second thoughts I think it best
> To stow it away in the old iron chest. (*groans*)

He used to declaim this when in a good humour, but we heard it rather often, because he knew little else. He would sing 'Mademoiselle from Armentières' and 'Pack up your Troubles in your Old Kit Bag', though; and also, to a jolly hornpipe tune:

> Oh I say Jack, have you ever seen the Queen?
> Have you ever seen a blue-bottle, in a submarine?
> From the heights of Gib-er-altar to the plains of sunny Malta,
> Will you have another drink before the boat comes in?

which is one thing I remember him singing to me on his knee when I was very small. My mother used light-heartedly to demur at this song: I suspect because the version I have set down above was Bowdlerized. It's what he sang though.

I believe that when I was a baby, my father used to dandle me on his knee and sing bawdy songs to me; which amused my mother though she thought them unsuitable for a first-born and man-child. My father hardly sensed a difference between what was bawdy and what was not. He had not suffered a 'dissociation of sensibility'. He had one or two rhymes he said to me, with the half-rhymes of the folk and the pronunciation of the folk on top of that: like 'tobacco' and 'matter'. In fact, he had learnt to say 'tobaccoo' and 'mattoo' in this particular rhyme: that was the tradition, and I was meeting the fact that in the popular mind it is reciting a poem that makes the words rhyme: not the rhyme that makes the poem.

My mother had a taste for what I cannot now help thinking a poor kind of Concert Song. She would beat out 'Seated One Day at the Organ' with great earnestness on the piano, and took the rich banal chords quite seriously. She also played 'Less . . . Then the Dust . . . Beneath Thy Chariot—Whee-eels! Less . . . than the Rust . . . that never Stains thy Sword! . . . Less . . . than the Trust . . . thou hast in me My Lo-ord! . . . Less . . . than all these . . . a-am I!' With this, as the second of a set of three, goes a lively piece which begins
     'The Temple Bells are Ri-i-nging!'
which she played with gusto. When she did this my father sometimes did one of his favourite tricks, which was to ring all the jugs, pots and cups on the table with the back of his knife. This made a gay if impudent and inharmonious accompaniment to the song. He used also to sing a version of his own to this song—only a line or so. I suspect it was very bawdy; and indeed the rhyme-scheme ('I lie sitting on the grass' was one of his lines . . .), as well as the silliness of the whole thing, invites nothing else. My mother, so far as I remember, quite enjoyed guying 'Temple Bells': but not 'Chariot Wheels'.

My mother used also to be fond of 'Hear My Prayer, O Lord incline Thine Ear': and this was a song sung at that time by a choir-boy who was justly celebrated for his voice, and

55

who could be heard often enough, singing this on the 'wireless' or on a gramophone in a shop or somewhere. In those days, by virtue of this song, he was the 'Top Ten' all by himself. Nor can I think of such pieces without valuing them, even now. Both my mother and I, from melodies and harmonies which I should now find trite and saccharine, took a deep and spontaneous joy which more sophisticated musical taste finds hard to match. The phrases that moved us became quickly, totally, easily, part of our consciousness. We could hum them, or hear them in our heads, the whole day long. They existed by themselves, endeared through intimacy and isolation. They did not have to take their place in a realm of systematized knowledge of the subject, knowledge reflected on, assessed, placed, even if enjoyed as well. I do not see how one can opt for naivety, but one cannot dismiss it either.

There was a more serious side to my mother's music, though it was not part of our culture as a family because it was more or less private to her. She played some of the quite difficult music of Chopin and Liszt and Schumann, and particularly got satisfaction from Rachmaninov's Prelude in C sharp minor. I stood by her for hours while she played. She knew most of the Rachmaninov by heart, and if she was practising it she wouldn't stop to light the gas; so we would be there in deep dusk in that room. As I grew older I could hear the note of proud, despairing anger in this piece; and I began to wonder what there was in my mother's life that I didn't know about, or at least understand, which drove her to play it over and over again with such absorption.

Besides many nursery rhymes, my mother passed on a number of traditional songs to me. 'Going A-Milking' was one which caught my attention as a small boy because of its last lines: 'And now she is the lawyer's wife . . . . . . rest of her life/ In a station greatly above her'. This repeated the sentiment I had found in the catechism. She also sang 'We Are the Roman Soldiers', and knew that the Romans once occupied Britain, though she had no ground for linking that fact, as she did, with the song. Another song was 'The Jolly Miller', and she pointed out to me, when I learned the piano with her, that this was an odd song because it seemed a gay one, yet the tune was in the minor. And she knew 'A Dusky Night Rides down the Sky' and 'The Old Man's Clock' and one or two others. All these songs, that she knew by popular oral tradition (she had learnt some of them from Edith, her mother's servant), she sang with easy spontaneity and gusto. 'What Shall he have who killed the Deer' and 'Under the Greenwood Tree' she had learnt as rounds with her father, and sang rather more self-consciously. She knew that the words were by Shakespeare, but otherwise Shakespeare meant little to her at this time. She did, however, know 'Fidele's Song', and found its sentiments true and moving. As I said, that sort of gentle Stoicism offered a good deal to people in her way of life.

My father knew few stories; his own childhood had not helped him to it. He read aloud to me sometimes, but he did not do that easily (he had left school when he was eleven). By the time I was six I could read from my own books almost as fluently as he could aloud. This fact surprised and rather saddened me, as I began to understand why it was: though it was not till I was ten or eleven, outside the time and the world of this book, that I really took stock of all that life had denied him—and some sides of this I could not really take stock of until later still.

So my father did not read to me very often, and when he told me stories they were likely to be those he had learned from hearing my mother. She read to me very often. What I remember best is *Grimm's Fairy Tales*, and some of these (like 'The Youth Who Wanted to Learn to Shiver') used to thrill her a good deal herself. She used to read Grimm to herself sometimes, and this shows her good taste.

We also had *The Blue Fairy Book* (Andrew Lang's I suppose) but it meant little to us because we thought all the best stories were in Grimm. When I was six, I think, I was given Hawthorne's *Tanglewood Tales*. It was too difficult for

57

me then, but about a year later I read a good deal of it, and the
Medusa story became very vivid to me, and one or two others
like Atlas. But this was something I did by myself. My mother
read to me from *East of the Sun—West of the Moon*, a book
which had very evocative *art nouveau* illustrations, and I learnt
about trolls and polar bears from it.

One part of the culture I drew from my mother was weather-
lore. I learnt when to look for a rainbow, and to look also for
the 'double bow'; and she could show me that the outer one
was reversed from the inner—though she didn't know why.
She showed me the little halo that forms round the moon, and
the marvellous great halo too; and she taught me to recognize
thunderheads (which we called 'anvil clouds'), told me how a
'mackerel sky' means fine weather, and explained how to tell
when a fine day would be wet before evening.

Much of her weather-lore was in rhyme:

> A red sky at night
> Is the shepherd's delight;
> Red sky at morning
> The Shepherd's warning.

This was one, and another was:

> Ash before oak
> And we shall have soak;
> Oak before ash
> And we shall have splash.

I learned that if it rained on St. Swithin's Day it would rain for
forty days after: this was very much one, in our minds, with the
forty days of the Flood. I learnt too about March: 'In like a
Lion, out like a Lamb'. I learnt that green in the sky meant wind
(Dickens puts this into the Peggotty part of *David Copperfield*).

My mother also taught me to look for the 'Harvest Moon'
and the 'Hunter's Moon', and told me that there was the
'Trapper's Moon' too, but she didn't know when it was. She

knew of 'St. Martin's Little Summer' and 'St. Luke's Little Summer' and the 'Indian Summer'; but couldn't tell exactly when each came. She could find the Great Bear and the Pleiades, and Mars (the red planet), Venus and on the whole Jupiter. She showed me eclipses of the moon, and in 1927, when a total eclipse of the sun was visible at London, tried to show me that; but we spent so long making dark glass by smoking it in a candle-flame, that we barely saw a thing. I can just remember the intense black disc in the sky. There was too much candle-smoke for us to see anything of the grandeur and strangeness of a solar eclipse as you read about it. So I shall probably never see that. She wasn't taking any chances with my eyes, that's what did it.

Besides our weather-rhymes, we had proverbs. There were quite a number of these and we took them quite seriously. They were truths about the facts of life, vouched for by their traditional nature, and at the same time with a clear call to our feelings—heartening, admonitory or prescriptive. 'It's a long lane that has no turning' was our most often quoted proverb: one can see why. But we also knew 'his bark's worse than his bite' and 'spoil the ship for a ha'porth of tar', and 'fine feathers make fine birds', which we used in a special sense, almost the opposite of what it says—I mean, to reject outsides, not endorse them as the road to worldly success. There were a number of other; but of course, by comparison with communities truly rich in proverbial lore, we were disinherited indeed.

We knew, for example, only one pair in which each could cap the other: 'too many cooks spoil the broth' and 'many hands make light work'. My mother and father exchanged these acrimoniously from time to time. But all the same, the proverb was still an accepted part of the residual folk-culture to which we belonged. Proverbs were all *true*.

At another level we had a stock of riddles, jokes and rudimentary word-games; and here our traditional culture made a link with our world of 'mass-communications'; for it could be supplemented, or kept familiar, by what we found in newspapers or children's Christmas annuals and the like. Some of our nursery rhymes had, of course, a game that went with them.

> There's the church
> And there's the steeple,
> Open the doors, and there's the people.

—this goes with showing what is happening by folding one's hands together in various ways.

> Two little dicky-birds
> Sitting on a wall;
> One named Peter,
> The other named Paul;
> Fly away Peter!
> Fly away Paul!
> Come back Peter,
> Come back Paul.

This is a rhyme-game my mother taught me, with two bits of stamp-paper stuck on her finger-nails to be the two birds. In lines 6 and 7 of the rhyme, one twirls one's hands in the air, and puts down, to show on the table, not the two finger-tips with the 'birds', but the two next ones; in the closing lines the birds come twirling back again. My mother could do it with just enough *bravura* to leave me guessing for a long time how she managed it.

She also taught me how to tap people's knees so as to make the reflex jerk, and how to poise my leg on the ball of my foot until it dithered up and down. Both of these came perhaps from having been a nurse: the latter is vastly amusing if you are about six. Besides this, she taught me how you can stop your teeth chattering with the cold, by making an effort, or let it get more and more till you almost feel your face is falling apart. This is also fun, except that you have to be cold into the bargain.

'Why is spring the most dangerous time of the year?' was

one of our riddles: the answer is, 'because the trees are shooting, and the bull-rush is (bull rushes) out!' That ran in the family: even my grandmother, who didn't smile often, smiled at that, and liked to tell it me. There were a handful of others. My mother also taught me to decipher:

If        the

# B

M        T

:

If        the

# B

m        T

;

which is about putting 'colon' and so forth, if the 'grate be' empty (M T), or 'a little empty' (mT). All readers of my own age will know these items of harmless nonsense. But to my parents these things were not just an amusement for the small child. They amused them a little too, and all in all they were a quite appreciable part of the things their minds were stored with, the mental things they could do. They did not have these for me, and Shakespeare or Karl Marx, in a separate compartment, for themselves. I think the same was true of many families.

I want to say a little about our material culture. We had some skills, and my parents passed them on to me. My mother taught me, very insistently, how to keep every part of myself clean (including my nails, about which many distinguished people know less than the cat). She showed me the right, and wrong, ways to brush my teeth. She scrupulously got rid of fleas with Keatings' Powder, and avoided lice (some boys at school had these from time to time, or at least she thought so) by meticulously regular use of a special fine comb—although she never found any. I learnt from her how to make a parting, tie a tie-knot (she had to work this out as she showed me), put iodine on cuts at once although it hurt a lot, spread butter over a burn, bandage over a joint—a knee, say; not un-freeze too fast if I got very cold, tie double bows to keep my shoes done up, button my coat the opposite way from a girl's, blow in my gloves to warm my hands, put my finger over a half-tied knot so as to finish it, use a bone shoe-horn for new shoes, and always cut things so that the knife moved away from my other hand. When I was very small I had fingerless gloves on an elastic through the sleeves of my coat, so as not to lose them. I also learnt how to get a splinter out with a needle, and several things to do to get things out of people's eyes. My father knew about this too: he was specially good, better than my mother, when you got something in your eye, though you had to be unfalteringly co-operative.

My mother also taught me how to make what I now consider impossibly strong tea ('one for each person, and one for the pot'), and cocoa. We never had coffee, except Camp coffee sometimes. The tea was something I was expected to learn, but not cooking—that wasn't a job for a male—though I was ever so often at her side while she was doing it. She herself was a good plain cook, especially with pies and puddings; her cakes were usually good but sometimes the fruit sank, and really she knew only two or three baking recipes. She also taught me how to make a bed, clean windows, and wash up expediously. She showed me how to wipe up three plates at a time (you keep moving them down, wiping the top and bottom of a set of three all the time). And she taught me how to darn socks, though she did it very well and I do it atrociously. She thought I might need that, but I never have.

Mainly she showed me how to put plants in, which became one of the few manual skills I feel I have by instinct. Besides this, though, she taught me a few things about drawing—like how to do 'stick' men—and how to begin on the proper side when you are doing a painting, how to keep your brushes clean and so forth. She also knew how to 'put a wash on', but I didn't really master this in my earlier childhood.

It is really quite difficult to unearth one's trivial skills. They feel almost like breathing, not part of a learned culture, and of course this whole account is very incomplete. From my father I learnt less than from my mother, but I learnt a good few things. One was something of how to draw animals, especially their heads and legs. He was quite good about horses' legs, and dogs' too, which he knew how to make quite different from horses'. He showed me the right place to punch someone's jaw (I've never done it), and a few more things like that, and how to kick a football and how to dribble it, which he was very good at. He didn't have much idea about cricket. He also taught me the rudiments of using carpenter's tools: hammer, chisel, plane, and how to put in screws with a gimlet, or do counter-sinking for the heads with a brace and bit. Also, more or less, I learnt how to look after chickens, pigeons, rabbits and the cat. He had many other manual skills. He used to build his own wireless sets from blue-prints that you could buy in those days; and he built several—the delicate soldering especially impressed me—from a crystal set with a 'cat's whisker' and ear-phones (we heard the second day of B.B.C. broadcasting on this) up to a seven-valve 'superhet' for which he also made an imposing three-legged cabinet which he 'French-polished'. That was another thing he could do. He was a good carpenter, and could do faultless dove-tail jointing. I remember how deeply he used to breathe, with his mouth slightly open, as he worked.

Our seasonal cycle was very restricted and attenuated. At Christmas we thought it essential to decorate the house with paper chains and bells and with berried holly (which we never bought, but foraged for). We put up mistletoe as well (it seemed not uncommon in those days), but it had nothing to do with kissing in our house, though it did elsewhere, like those Firemen. It was also essential to stuff the Christmas Day chicken (though two or three times we had pork as a substitute, because we couldn't afford the chicken) and you also had

to have bread sauce. There had to be a Christmas pudding with
a holly sprig on it and a silver threepenny piece inside (this was
always manœuvred my way). My mother made a fruit cake,
iced it with white icing sugar (that looked like snow, of course),
and put a little china reindeer and Father Christmas on top.
These were packed away, and reappeared each year. Hazels,
walnuts, brazil-nuts, almonds and a box of dates—never more
than one—were necessary if Christmas was to be properly kept.
We did not have them at any other time. So were mince-pies,
dusted with castor sugar. There was nothing to drink, save of
course strong tea. My parents exchanged small gifts and also
Christmas cards, and hung a stocking (they were generous:
sometimes it was a pillow-case) at the foot of my bed. I think
I was five-and-a-half before I learnt that Santa Claus and his
reindeer were a fiction. I'm glad to say I thought it was much
nicer that my parents did it themselves.

We also had a box of Christmas crackers, and the mottoes
and riddles inside to some extent fed our fund of silly word-
games. One year we had about eight boxes, marvellous
expensive crackers, large and small, thick and thin, in every
variety of shiny or velvety paper. They would have cost
pounds, even then: but they came to us in a staff share-out
from the hospital. We also had a Christmas tree with decorations but without gifts on it. Like the cake, it had some
decorations which reappeared each year; but many of them
turned up from time to time in what my father brought home.
My mother taught me 'Good King Wenceslas', one or two
other familiar carols, and also one or two Christmas hymns,
which we sang vigorously together. She was very insistent
that I learned 'Come All Ye Faithful', and 'Hark the Herald
Angels Sing', exactly the way they are in the hymn-book.
People usually sing the tunes wrong. Occasionally carol-
singers came to the door, but only children in twos and threes.

We almost never went to church at Christmas, but we knew
about the 'watch-night' service at St. Mark's, and sometimes
we got as far as to think of going. That church had no church-

yard, its walls were straight on the street. When you passed it at night in sparkling dark winter frost, you could see the mellow light from the stained-glass chancel windows, and it looked very warm and cosy inside, but this was emphatically not so. St. Mark's was 'High' and had a little red light which 'never went out', and so filled me with awe.

On New Year's Eve my parents (and when I was seven or eight I with them) stayed up to 'see the Old Year out and the New Year in', and listened to Big Ben on the wireless—with one earphone apiece, at first. This was again an occasion without alcohol, and the family went to bed, without contacting its neighbours, at five minutes past midnight. Then, as the year advanced, we tried to have pancakes on Shrove Tuesday; we knew about Lent though we did not observe it; and I remember learning also about Advent, and being surprised that for this, there wasn't even something that in fact you didn't do after all

For Easter, we thought you had to have hot-cross buns on Good Friday, and Easter-eggs on Sunday. I knew all about what Christmas and Easter meant, but not Whitsun. Side by side with shop eggs in chocolate or marzipan (this I adored) we sometimes had hens' eggs for Easter Sunday; my mother painted them red or blue with paint from my paint-box: but we had really lost this custom, and didn't know how to make a show with it—besides, we were too small a family.

April 1st was a real April Fools' Day: my mother and I played April Fool on my father, and sometimes, though not often, he did to her; and the road was full of the children playing harmless tricks on the adults. At All Saints' School we could play April Fools until noon, and after that used to be told more and more firmly to come-along-now and stop it. One mark of the loathsome and vicious school to which I went for a year when I was eight was that on March 31st we were solemnly warned, by the headmaster walking round from class to class with his cane as usual hooking up over his lapel, that the slightest observance of this custom on the day following would be met with the only form of communication with children that that degraded little sadist understood. In this school, though, as in the one I went to from nine to eleven, the really vicious beatings were strictly on a class basis. I can still remember the chief victims: Singer from Coventry Road with his crop-head (he was the eldest of five, and mothered the others, he called them 'my littluns'); Trott with his father's trousers, cut down but much too big; Timmis with his jacket that had lasted too long and was far too small, Ridout with his dark brown eyes as soft as a deer's. They were all the poorest boys in the class. Perhaps they got the same at home or worse: the teacher thought it didn't matter. I can also remember our astonishment when a quite nice (though irascible) master brutally savaged one of the industrious and fairly clever boys from a respectable middle-class family. This was because, having received a mark of four for an exercise, he turned the figure into a face, and labelled it with the master's name. More work for the gallows-builders.

Well . . . there was little more, really, to our annual cycle in so far as it based itself on the family. On May-day we felt happy and admired the May blossom—if it was out. Sometimes we picked it, but it was deadly unlucky to bring it indoors. Sometimes children carried flags in the streets on 'Empire Day' (young people will not even know the date of it now). Then the year was featureless until Harvest-festival time, when my mother and I used to go into St. Mark's Church sometimes to see the fruits and vegetables—there would be ever so many, from all the allotments everywhere I suppose. Two or three times we went to the Harvest Festival Service. We used to watch the swallows gathering to leave (the swallows and the cuckoo were the only migrants we could see in a place like South Norwood, but we noticed them each year), and if there were a lot of scarlet hips and crimson haws, my mother would predict a severe winter.

A proper display of November 5th fireworks had to include bangers, catherine-wheels, and at least one rocket. The poorer boys had 'guys' in the streets, and sometimes turnip-heads with a candle inside (the Hallowe'en custom: but I didn't know about Hallowe'en). Families like my own, though, had nothing to do with this. Having a guy on 'wheels' went with asking for money; and they used to use those same wheels, those boys, to go round the street collecting the horse-dung for their fathers' gardens. I wasn't allowed wheels. You often saw a householder rush out of his front door with a shovel to scoop up after a horse in those days. There was no abundance of wood in our district, but nevertheless we several times had a fire, and what is more we made and burnt a 'guy' as well. Once at least our guy was so well made, so life-like and lovable, that I was very sad at his going.

There has been a big change about Guy Fawkes. I learnt about Guy Fawkes and his gunpowder barrels from my parents, when I was just five. They didn't know about the 'Popery' side to the story, or if they did they didn't care; but otherwise it was very real to them.

> Please to remember
> The Fifth of November
> Gunpowder treason and plot;
> And I see no reason
> Why Guy Fawkes's treason
> Should ever be forgot.

It was my father I learnt this from, not my mother. She knew it, of course, but it was so familiar to everyone that he knew it too.

The last day marked in the annual cycle, before Christmas came again, was Armistice Day. It was marvellous. In those years, the war of 1914–1918 was still on everyone's lips. The poppy-sellers would be everywhere in the morning. Quite ordinary lower middle-class people spent a shilling (more like five today) and wore a grandiose vermilion firework of a poppy in their lapel for the rest of the day. Then came eleven o'clock and the two minutes' silence. Everything stopped.

Everyone stood still in the streets. The men took off their hats, like a funeral. (You always stood still with your hat off, in those days, as a hearse passed: but of course, there was more to it than there is now, because of the four black horses, stepping gravely and slowly, and at their ears, sable-dyed ostrich plumes that waggled as they went.)

The buses drew in to the side and the drivers got out and stood to attention. The silence was like a great, sudden, invisible ocean all round. You could see not one movement, nor hear a sound save the far-away boom of the maroons at Woolwich. Once we heard an ambulance—it might have been miles away—that drove on right through the two minutes, its bell-clang something beyond belief as it grew louder, stayed the same for a little, then slowly died away. Save for this one time, the silence and stillness were complete. The whole thing was a real contact, for one day in the year, with grandeur, solemnity and tragedy—a whole nation had a single common feeling. Now there is nothing like it.

Another side of the culture seems to me now rather strange. In a sense, it was our mythology. We belonged to the working-class-middle-class fringe that had no politics, and so our sense of public affairs centred on the Royal Family, not the political parties. But it was royalty from a special point of view: not simply, not so much even, the dignified respectability of trim-bearded George V and his stately deep-bosomed consort, but something more primitive, more barbaric. 'The King can do no wrong!', my father taught me with emphasis. He believed it firmly, though he could not have elaborated it. But for him it wasn't in the slightest degree a legal fiction. Beyond this, royalty meant the Crown itself, and the Crown Jewels, which we had seen in the barbaric setting of that medieval fortress, the Tower of London.

In fact, what surrounded kingship for us was, almost more than anything else, a dim idea of severity and violence. My mother taught me about the Two Little Princes in the Tower. I knew, from very early on, about King Charles I and his head.

Above all, I had been told of the massacre of the Czar's whole family in a cellar in snowy Siberia. Communists meant nothing, but this extermination of a whole imperial line meant so much, it began to have a hint of the trauma. And I had stared, through its glass case, at the block in the Tower. The King didn't use that block any more, but it was his all the same.

And in things like this, I think, lay the main part of our mythology; if by that word is meant a community's sense of the great external forces which set bounds to their lives and may intervene in them, at any time, with tragic finality. Our sense of the world beyond ourselves owed little or nothing to religion, politics or social science, and it took shape instead in our images of the criminal law, the courts, and the machinery of punishment. One minor part of this was the talk about boys who fell into the hands of the police and 'got the birch'. I hardly knew what this was, but it was some awe-ful thing. Nearer to the centre were handcuffs, the Black Maria, hard labour, the second division, the broad arrow, penal-servitude-for-life, Broadmoor, and Dartmoor, all granite, where gangs of convicts worked on the moors, in the rain all day, under armed guards. All this I could relate to the barred basement window in the Police Station in the High Street: that was 'the cells'. My father was very much afraid of the police, though he never did anything worse than cycle without a light. He did this pretty often though.

But the heart of our mythology of fear and fascination was murder and the gallows. In those times, a murder could take up most of the front page of the popular press day after day. The trials were reported in every detail. The sense was of a great machine slowly but irresistibly tracking down the murderer. Murders themselves seemed saner, more calculated, more cold-blooded than they do now: seemed more to issue (as perhaps they did) from normal feelings driven, over long periods, to desperation. I heard of the great Poisoners—Dr. Crippen, Mrs. Bywater and her lover, and the rest. 'Arsenic' was a magic term: one thought about it and was afraid. Then came the arrests, with pictures in the papers of a figure bundled along with his head muffled in a coat. Then the trial and— usually it seemed—the gloomy rituals that followed. I had never seen any of this, but we all three knew about it. I can still hear my father's uneducated voice quoting '. . . And may the Lord have mercy on thy Soul'. He and my mother knew the judge's whole formula more or less by heart. We thought with awe about the black cap, the condemned cell, the trap opening, the hangman's knot behind the left ear, the black flag going up over Wandsworth gaol, the man coming down to fix the notice to the prison gate, being buried in quicklime. I learned, very young, what had happened to Mrs. Bywater when she was hanged along with her lover*; and how this had made the powers that be resolve (what was not, I am sorry to say, the case) at least never to hang a woman again. Some of all this was probably quite out with the facts. But the mythology of the gallows had its power all the same—for our family and doubtless for a million others.

Perhaps it will surprise some readers that I have written so long about our culture, and not yet mentioned our code of values, our morality. The fact is that this did not press on us. We easily lived within its demands. It was there all right though. We didn't, of course, have need of a taboo against homicide; but we had an ultimate taboo against thieving money or most of the things with a plain money value—new clothes, shop goods, jewellery. At the other extreme were things like bits of wood left lying about and good for firing, which you had no need to think twice about—though not of course from someone's wood-pile. My mother also had no scruple over the odd garden-plant, especially if you could get it without 'setting foot' on someone else's land (you surprisingly often can). Even so, she would have thought it wrong to take all that a man

---

* I ought to note that I learned all the 'facts of life', from my mother, so young that even as a child I could never remember when I had anything still to learn. The only exception was certain details about homosexuality, which were not explained to me until the Arbuckle case of 1930.

had of any given kind, or more than three or four altogether. This way, you could get some plants, but not stock your garden; and of course not do it at all to sell—that was like stealing money. Taking from public or semi-public stocks was different again: you could have a bit of sand, say, from the roadman's pile, or possibly (though this would have been rather borderline) enough coal just to keep you going, if you'd run right out, from a big dump like the one at the station. You could also have a bit of orchard fruit, or field-turnips out in the country; but not garden things like currants (even from that derelict kitchen garden, the currants left me ill at ease). In every doubtful case, the boundary was the point at which the owner might begin to sense his loss in money terms.

In all this, of course, we knew there was a difference between the conventional respectability, and the point at which our own moral feelings really began to come into play. So—it seems to me now—my parents did with sexual morality. Flirting and 'vamping' were frowned on, but if even a married man or woman were 'carrying on' seriously with someone, this was not wholly to their discredit, perhaps slightly the reverse in that often it went with liveliness and outgoingness, which we mildly admired. But they had to avoid gossip, and they certainly had not to grow remiss in looking after their spouse or house or children; otherwise it was very bad. On the other hand, 'wronged' spouses who became violent were not commended or sided with, but were not condemned either. They had a sort of right to add trouble to trouble if they felt that way. The others had 'asked for it'. In fact, we had about these matters the sense which makes possible the art-form of tragedy —men and woman will be as they are, and things will go as they must. This was also our attitude to girls who got babies and the fathers who threw them out—neither could much be blamed. Some sexual offences seemed really bad though. Being 'loose' (very promiscuous) was unsavoury, and if a woman of some age had a very young lover, it was a little unsavoury. An older man could more easily 'carry on' with a much younger woman, but it at once became very bad if he tricked her or exploited her inexperience. On the other hand, while 'seducers' (who could only be males) aroused very strong feelings, my parents had also a pretty shrewd idea that it was possible to be, as it were, more seduced against than seducing. 'She led him on' could express a lot.

It was also nasty if a man was effeminate or a woman mannish, but the matter of homosexuality never really came our way save as one form of offences against children. These were the only sexual things that really outraged my parents (incest and one or two other comparable things never entering their experience). They aroused the strongest feelings of mystified horror and incipient rage, and they had nothing whatever to do with being ill. No one had thought of that. Judged in the abstract, I think my parents would have thought hanging inappropriate (in part on account of its mythological association with murder) but not any other form of severity, at least any form then practised in England.

But all this merely adds up to the fact that in their straight-forward way, my parents had hold of one major truth: that 'sexual morality' is not a fundamental concept at all, since real sexual evil is evil because it includes an evil which can equally well show itself elsewhere. Perhaps the thing that they most sharply saw the evil of was cruelty. They knew quite well that it need not be physical, and for both my father and my mother it included cruelty to animals as well as people, though he was a good deal more no-nonsense about that than she was. To be a bully, whatever it was to, was among the worst things. Far short of that, though very bad too, were deception and lie-telling in order to benefit yourself through harm to someone else. But there were also 'white lies', and deceiving a 'Nosy Parker' was quite all right; in fact, it was one of the times when you could do a bit of 'kidding' if you were up to it. Spitefulness, malicious envy and 'back-biting' were major vices, greediness and conceit substantial ones, meanness over money far from trivial ('misers' were a part of our mythology), ill-temper disagreeable, but not a fault unless it led to something else. Being narrow-minded and 'fault-finding' was much worse.

I put first the things we condemned, because they bulked the larger in our thoughts. First, on the other side, I think must come meeting the special claims that others could make on you. You had to do your job and take care of your family: the obedience of children was their return for being housed and fed and—an important addition—taught how to behave. On the other hand, there were limits to this: there came a point when a child could say, 'I didn't *ask* to be born'. I gathered that my mother had often felt like saying it. We also had a quite strong idea of the duties of friendship (though we had, all three of us, few friends)—especially of what it was right to do for, or suffer from, one's 'best friend'. Looking back, I am surprised at the strength of this very traditional concept in our thoughts.

Next came the capacity to rise to the occasion in a crisis. Above all, this meant being strong when things went wrong. You could complain and lament (though better if you didn't) but had to be brave in the end, and do what fell to you. Those around you had to be generous, and helpful, to forbear or forgo, in a way that would have been unnecessary or even troublesome in the normal course of things. Our morality had no place for saints, and 'keeps himself to himself' was praise. But in crisis or catastrophe, one 'went out of one's way'; that was the phrase.

Courage was an important virtue, and in large part or perhaps in the main it meant physical courage. A man who met the just claims of others on him, and also knew how to be uncomplaining and brave, was well on the way to superiority. But to be a truly superior man, he had to add to that a certain dignity and imperturbability of manner; which were much more serious goods than liveliness and outgoingness, though they had to be free from 'starchiness'. He also had to add 'manners'. For my mother and also my father (though in different ways) 'manners' were very important. I think they were for our neighbours too. How to eat was quite important, but the most important things, on the whole, were to do the right things when you met people or said goodbye to them; to go on being polite (at least for a long time) when others were rude; and to behave properly to women. These were enough, in our small and eventless world. For children, it was also important to defer properly to adults. Where this morality of manners went beyond forms was with guests. For them, one had a special responsibility, which called for qualities like sympathetic response, perceptiveness and self-effacingness (though we by no means knew their names). This was quite a strict part of the code: one's sole remedy was that sooner or later a guest was sure to go, and 'you needn't ask him again . . .'

Clearly the 'manners' part of our code was shallow, and as a whole our values were limited. We had little sense of group loyalty, 'belonging', gaiety in common, or political responsibility; as we should, had we been a real working-class family. In general our way of life was much too withdrawn and private: at bottom, we had no defence whatever against political evil, and in this (as the events of the late 1930s showed) were like millions of our compatriots. We had still, perhaps, some attenuated contact with a traditional ideal, that of the kind of sceptical sagacity which belongs to the common people. Phrases like 'I don't know so much', 'take the wind out of his sails', or 'know a trick worth two of that' were often on our lips. But just as we lacked the working-class ideals, so we did those of others much above us: ambitious culture; intellectual or emotional distinction; tolerance, reticence, comprehension. The disciplined development of life meant little more for us than avoiding hypocrisy on the one hand, or silliness on the other. But for all this, our code warranted respect. It met most, though not all, of the limited opportunities and limited demands which our condition of life held out to us; and there was little in it that was silly, and nothing that was either self-righteous or barbarous: which is more than can be said of most codes, if the truth be told.

74

# Chapter six

# Toy soldiers and others

A few of my toys came from Street's, the toyshop in Portland Road; but most of them came in quite another way. My father brought them home from Queen's Hospital. Sometimes they would come in a box he would tie, with what seemed a lot of string, on his bicycle: of course he had to tie the box on well, because he had a long way to come. But it used to take a long time to get that string off, especially since we seldom cut it. Instead, it went into my mother's string-drawer (we bought our first ball of string when I was about eight, we saved so much in bits and pieces). Once or twice my father brought toys home in a sack or a bag on his back. These times he had to ride one-handed. I thought in those days, and I still think, that my father by no means loved me the way my mother did: but he was an affectionate man, and was attached to me, and also it gave him a strong, perhaps rather youthful kind of pleasure, to be the giver.

So I had a great many toys of certain kinds: far more than went with our resources. These were toys that were given to the hospital and were not thought right for the children who were patients; or they were passed on to the staff for their own children when there was a glut. And sometimes, I think, when a big supply of toys arrived at the hospital and there was a large-scale hurried share-out, the workmen got hold of toys that they might have got, or might not, if the sister in charge (or whoever it was) had had eyes all round her head. If my father was good and quick at this I am grateful to him, and when I think of the world he lived in (I was all right) and what he had in life, I honour him for it. And if he ever actually stole toys for me I feel the same but more so. And if I didn't, I'd not admit it.

At all events, if there was a share-out, toys had to be brought away in a hurry: either because if they lay about the other men might take them, or because some less amiable member of the staff might see what was going on and want to take something back. Once my father came home knowing there would be a share-out, and we spent the whole day trying to find or borrow the biggest cardboard box we could get, so that he could take it and fill it. Usually the toys would be shared out in the afternoon or evening, and this meant that my father brought away his winnings when he left at 10 o'clock. And I think also that the workmen made a point of leaving with large parcels when they were leaving in the dark—such things came like an instinct to the working class, even when there was no need.

But when he left Hackney at 10 o'clock it would be far later than that before he got home with the toys. So the impression I have now is of my toys arriving in the dead of night. I would hear the key bustle in the door, and the purr of his bicycle tyres on the linoleum in the hall (he kept it under the stairs), and the ticking sound of his three-speed gear; then the noise and talk, and the light in the hall would go on, and they would let me wrap up in a blanket and go down. My father was not one to postpone the pleasure of watching me with the toys until morning; so several times there were great sessions that lasted an hour or so, when the world outside was dark and asleep and very quiet. Then I would go back to bed. If he was on nights, the toys might come with the sun.

From the hospital came the first special toy I had and one I always loved a great deal: a red wooden engine that I used to ride up and down the kitchen when I was very small; and I also acquired a large number of woolly animals. I never went in for dolls (some boys do), but in the end I had twenty-seven animals (rabbits, bears, a jerboa, an elephant, woollen birds and the like). All of them fitted into a strict order of precedence, but I took care of even the twenty-seventh of them, according to that station to which it had pleased Providence to call it; and played with my animals after most boys give up such things.

Another thing I used to get a lot of were children's Christmas Annuals. I don't know if this kind of book is very much seen today. They were popular when I was a child—big illustrated children's books, with stories, and jokes and puzzles, and many pictures large and small; the whole thing was somehow made Christmassy, and used for children's presents at Christmastime, but meant I suppose to last all through the year. Well, by the end of January the first lot of children had got tired of them and they went to the hospitals, and by the spring—or sometimes the same day—they found their way into the hands of the hospital staff. Most of them were brought out by the publishers of children's picture comics, and carried on the stories that came in these week by week—usually with animal characters like Tiger Tim, in those far-off, naive times. I had many of these annuals at an age when pictures impressed me far more than writing. Many years later, in my thirties, I was turning over the pages of one that my mother had fetched out from the bottom of the trunk where she kept her treasures, and my eye fell on one picture, in an orange-brown tint, of a path going down, between trees and bushes on either side, to some kind of castle gate. This caught my eye. I found it meaningful and evocative as nothing else in the book was still. Then I realized that one of the most deeply and lyrically felt of the recurrent dreams I had had over many years, and well into my twenties, was simply the dream of walking into this picture and down this road into the castle at the end. Of course, dreams like that probably link up with something else besides childhood books.

This is perhaps the place to write about my sleeping life as a child. I often went to bed, not by gaslight, but a candle in an iron candlestick enamelled pale green. It stood on the corner of my mother's dressing-table, and threw high shadows in warm brown round the room. The bars of my cot (my father had made it, and stained it with permanganate of potash, so it was purplish) made shadows that rose almost to the ceiling. I used to look at how the shadow of the bar at the top twisted when it crossed the corner of the room. I can still see my mother's face bright, but the rest of her in shadow, as she blew the candle out; and still hear the quick puff she made. Then the dark used to seem to rush at my eyelids, quick, heavy, velvety, noiseless. It seemed a thick, active thing, seemed almost to pick me up and hold me. But after a few minutes the faint light from outside would begin to show dully at the edges of our old green blinds; and then the dark would just be the dark.

It wasn't the case that I found the dark frightening. My chief fear in the darkness was not of the dark itself, but something very odd: it was that *a lord* would come. I don't mean the Messiah, I mean simply an English nobleman. I was very much afraid of lords. I had never met or even seen one, of course, but I had got the idea from somewhere that they were arrogant and pitiless men, as well as martial and dashing, and would have no scruple in bringing the most awful punishments and disasters down on ordinary people who aroused their displeasure. It occurs to me that these ideas may have grown up from something my mother said as she was thinking about Dumas' *The Man in the Iron Mask*. We didn't have this book, but she remembered it.

I used also to see streams of hypnagogic images—these are the kind that come in the dark across one's open eyes. I used to see dozens of faces, moving swiftly in lines, all ugly, all greyish-brown from being in deep shadow, all staring at me. Fortunately, the very first time this happened, I realized that it was like a bad dream when you could tell yourself it was only a dream all the time; so I wasn't frightened of these faces, though I can't deny that the interest with which they filled me was an anxious kind of interest.

I found that consciousness could take other strange forms in the dark, if you didn't fall asleep quickly. One was a curious making simple of the sense of touch, so that it reported all objects under a simple two-fold division, just rough or smooth. My cot-bars, the sheets, my skin and I think the wall gave the one feel, and the blankets, the hot-water-bottle cover, and the mat (I could reach down through the bars to it) the other. I used to grope round in the dark trying every texture I could find to see which of the two feels it had. Neither of them was exactly like anything feels to normal touch. There were one or two things which refused to fit into the pattern; if I touched them, the spell was broken and normal touch returned. One was cold glass. But on the whole I used to avoid these: I didn't want the spell broken. That also happened at once if I climbed out of bed, except once or twice. These were very odd times indeed.

But the oddest change that used to happen to me in the dark was one that I still find it very hard to put into words. It was just that, quite suddenly, there would be a small but total change in my whole consciousness, a change so elusive (though so decisive) that once when I tried to ask my mother about it, she simply couldn't understand what I was trying to say. When this happened I felt more clear-headed than usual—but I found, on the other hand, that I couldn't understand or solve anything which normally was beyond me. I felt as if time were racing, yet at the same time as if it were going with a curious hurried deliberateness. I felt more tense and expectant than usual, and yet also more composed and serene. This wasn't something that affected merely the senses: the seat of con-

79

sciousness itself appeared to shift. I felt like another person, though in close continuity with myself. I used to wonder if there were those who felt this way all day long—for whom this was the normal state. To a limited extent I learnt to throw myself into this condition of mind;* and at a cruder level, I found I could also 'make my head go round' in the dark. But I used to be pretty careful about this. You had to switch it off before too late, or it felt as if you might start to spin at top speed and never stop.

In my later childhood, little by little, I lost all these propensities. But I still had nightmares. These were not particularly bad though they were quite bad enough: I wished them no worse and used to wake up sweating though not screaming. There were two kinds, the less bad non-recurrent ones that I could sometimes see had grown out of what I'd done or heard about recently, and the recurrent ones that felt as if they came from something much deeper down. There were four or five of these. It wasn't until many years later that I saw that they all had the same radical pattern: suddenly realizing you were very close to a big person who was watching you silently, with a kind of grim, treacherous-seeming good-humour. The worst was of a grey-haired, middle-aged woman in a pink jersey, looking down on me from high above and smiling a little cold smile. That was a knock-out nightmare.

What struck me, in later years, was that this radical pattern fitted quite closely with what a baby would see, if he got a fright from some stranger towering over his pram or cradle. My wife, who is a short woman, was delighted when I told her that I thought my nightmare radical was of a very tall one. When I was about thirty, and hadn't had those dreams for years, it happened that one day we were doing something which meant we were using the step-ladder, and by chance

* Many years later I found something which was just a little like this: getting drunk on too much black coffee, which is quite different from alcohol, and rather to be avoided as a sensation. Maybe what I felt as a child just came from too much tea.

she was wearing a pink pullover. She climbed up until she was like a woman seven feet high or so, and played my nightmare for me. Instantly, I had to ask her to stop, to come down, it wasn't any kind of a game that I could see—to my chagrin, and our amusement—but disquieted amusement—a moment later.

Well, but I began by writing about toys. I suppose my stamp album comes under this. I had a remarkable stamp album that came from Queen's Hospital, I should think when I was nearly seven. It had a good collection of stamps, too: not only many Victorian Colonial stamps, and a big set of 'Penny Browns' (there wasn't a Penny Black), but also some very beautiful stamps from pre-war Imperial China, Japan and Czarist Russia. The Russian Empire stamps were extraordinarily remote-looking, and beautiful too, in a delicate sharp filigree of black or deep blue. Unfortunately this collection was destroyed when I was eight, and early stamps like that never came my way again.

Another kind of toy that I had from Queen's, was toy soldiers: they were made of lead in those days, and some of them were made in solid lead. I had a lot of soldiers, and those from the hospital were reinforced, once or twice, with presents from other people. All in all, there were enough to make quite a presentable little army of British, unit by unit (each unit was six to fourteen strong), and I also had Gurkha soldiers whose shapely brown faces and lithe informal stances I especially liked. I learnt about the bravery of Gurkhas from my father. I also had several excellently made cannon, one complete with a gun-carriage and a shot that fired with a spring, and enough in the way of carts and waggons to make something of a baggage train. The enemy was always Red Indians, and I had a lot of these too, enough to make a fairly even battle, or for the Indians to win if only a few of the others mutinied and defected to them (I knew about mutinies from *Treasure Island*: my mother had read some of it aloud to me).

On both sides, the soldiers stood for me in a firmly fixed order of affection and preference, and I liked best the small,

neat, shapely ones. In my battles, the British usually won in the
end, but the Indians (save for the braves in especially violent
attitudes) had more of my sympathy, and the one I made
senior Indian chief—a skinny but intrepid-looking figure with
whom, doubtless, I identified myself—was an object of great
affection to me. In spite of what was really an aesthetic preference for dignified defensive attitudes among my soldiers, I
was fascinated by ideas of flank attacks, sudden raids, and
decisive breakthroughs; and also, at a very young age, I had
clearly formed ideas of a sort of chess-game of manœuvre,
until one side had gained a position of decisive advantage and
could attack and be sure to win. And I knew about patrols and
trench warfare. I must explain in a minute where I got these
ideas from. I saw no difficulty in having Red Indians take part
in trench warfare.

When my father was on early shift, my mother used to get
up at a quarter past four so as to get him off to work (then she
came back to bed: I knew because I used quite often to be
woken up by the slam of the door, and see her come quietly
back again). When he was on late shift, she usually stayed up
to wait for him to get home, and this would be between eleven
and midnight. All this meant that she slept short hours at
night, and she made up for it by having a 'rest' under the
eiderdown, with the blinds down, more or less every afternoon.
And I used to have to rest with her: I was out of trouble, and
also it was supposed to be good for me. I found the hills and
hummocks that her body made in the bed-clothes very good
for Red Indians to crawl over, and the deep parallel blanket-
folds made fine trenches for the British—or ravines for the
Indians. I did all this as gingerly as I could, and my mother
stayed dozing, or bore it, or did not bear it, as the case might be.

Sometimes my father brought very improbable oddments
home from Queen's—like, for example, a great bunch of
brown and white banded feathers. We thought they must be
eagle's feathers: but I now think they came from a turkey-
cock. With them, and an old piece of brown blanket that had

hung about for a long time, and that she fringed out at the edges, my mother made me a really splendid Redskin costume, which I wore for the first time to a fancy dress Christmas party at school when I was seven and a half. What thought, patience, labour she put into it! Of course I got—or she got— the first prize: that costume was almost embarrassingly good, too good for the occasion. The year after, she made me a pirate, in a shirt of patches of bright-coloured silk, and a silk cap that flopped over one eye—another reflection, all this, of *Treasure Island*. I can still see the clear red and golden yellow, and the dusty sheen of the silk, as if it had pollen on it. But both she and I realized that we could never again do as well as the Redskin.

But I was talking about playing soldiers, and what I knew about trench warfare. The source of all this was 'The World War'. 1914–18 hung over our house as I suppose it did over millions in those years. At about four, children begin to be clearly aware that there was a world, and that their parents had a life, before they themselves were born. So they start to explore these things by asking questions. For me, there could never be an answer, save one that brought in the Great War. It touched on everything. Little by little, as well as munition factories, rationing, blackouts, zeppelin raids and the rest, I began to get an idea of the B.E.F. and of life on the Western Front. First there was the photograph of my father in his puttees, with his horse. At one point in my childhood, someone showed us some pages from a newspaper during the Battle of the Somme—page after page after page, full of nothing but the names of the dead, in the smallest type I had ever seen. My father had been gassed with mustard gas, though only slightly. In the streets, in the 1920s, it was a common thing to see men with amputated legs or arms—you might see a half-dozen in a morning. Blind men, blind from mustard gas often enough, sang in the streets or sold matches or bootlaces from minute trays across their chests. Their stock was worth a half-crown maybe. They were not allowed to beg, so they had these things to sell and stood with their heads up proudly, soldier-wise;

and their caps out in their hands. Often, the street musicians were disabled servicemen. They used to plod along, puffing and banging, in their medals, not just the ribbons, but the real thing. They clanked sometimes. Then there were the pavement artists. One of these, with his crude patriotic drawings in garish blue, red and white crayon ( H.M. King George V, the *Hood*, Lord Kitchener, and so on), used to be up the station approach, by Portland Road bridge, whenever you went past. I think he was the one who sat on the stump of his leg, so for a long time I didn't know about it. Another used to have his picture-gallery up the slope just beyond the bridge: almost outside the man's lavatory. Nurse Cavell was dead—I knew about her all right—and the Kaiser was still alive in Holland. He was a little like—well, Cromwell to Irish children. My mother told me all about 'getting the white feather' if you weren't in uniform—it seemed the last degradation—and my father used a bandage to show me how to put on a puttee.

I knew quite a lot about the Great War; and I learnt it all from a single book. This was by far the most influential single object in my whole childhood. It was a large volume called 'The People's Atlas'. The sub-title was *The World Transformed*. I do not know if, handsomely and solidly bound in blue cloth, it came from Queen's Hospital, or if my mother or my father bought it. But it turned up when I was about six and could read fairly well. It literally fell to pieces in my hands between that age and nine or ten—I have it still, but the spine is off, and half the pages have come unsewn, while some are almost in tatters. This atlas is before me now, a wreck.

'The People's Atlas' reflects the spirit of that time. It opens with the Peace Treaty, and then the Covenant of the League of Nations . . . next there is a series of idealistic statements by the Great Men of the Peace Age—George V, Lloyd George (the picture of him is unusually engaging and teddy-bear-like), President Wilson, The Archbishop of Canterbury, Clemenceau ('The Tiger': I knew about him), the King of 'gallant little Belgium', and some more who are now forgotten. Then there is a facsimile of part of the Peace Treaty, with the seals, in reproduction, looking exactly like Mr. Blackman's pontefract cakes; and then, after the diagrams and maps, the 'Diary of the Making of War and Peace' (that kind of solemn style, which seems a little pinchbeck today, was everywhere then).

I pored over this diary by the hour. Some of it I couldn't understand, but much was quite easy . . . *'Hymn of Hate' first published at Munich . . . British stormed Hill 60*—my father had been at Hill 60, so I grasped that at once. I had to guess at the meaning, and indeed pronunciation, of 'asphyxiating' gas, but anyone could see it was the same as what my father talked about. There was the sinking of the *Lusitania*; Gallipoli (my father had still been mounted for that campaign); . . . *'Sinn Fein rebellion'*—I'd heard about the Sinn Fein from my mother, and the Black and Tans too. I, at least, thought to begin with that the Black and Tans were Irish extremists, and I think she half did too.

The double-column war diary went on, with its big pages of soft, almost woolly paper, the kind so popular at the time. *H.M.S. 'Triumph' torpedoed . . . H.M.S. 'Majestic' sunk . . . Battle of Jutland . . . the British Grand Fleet . . . German fleet saved from annihilation . . .* These naval engagements were perhaps the commonest things in the war films of the 1920s. We had seen the battle of Jutland at least twice, at the Central; and I at No. 6, and the little boy at No. 12, used to play at naval engagements, each mounted on our coal-sheds with a stick for a sixteen-inch gun. It fired a round every time you cried 'bang!': but you had to imagine the black smoke and the deep red flare belching from the muzzle. . . . *Germans made an attack with 'flame-throwers'.* My father described what a flame-thrower looked like at the hot end. He did not love the Germans. . . . *tanks brought into action for the first time . . . battle of Vimy Ridge . . . daylight raid on London by Gothas.* My father told me about the one, and my mother the other . . . *first moon-light air raid.* My mother could remember how the shrapnel rattled on the roofs, and the searchlights searched and searched but seldom found; my father could show me the scar on his leg where they'd taken out a piece of shrapnel as big as one of his horny fingers. *Paris shelled by 'Big Bertha' at a range of seventy miles.* We had an old newspaper photograph, grey and a bit tattered, of this gun. It must have been a fearsome legend to English civilians at the time; to my mother it was so still. Finally came the transformation of the war in the West during 1918 . . . *Great German offensive . . . Foch's brilliant counter-attack ('the turning of the tide') . . . 'Germany's Black Day' . . . Hindenberg line broken . . . Kaiser's flight to Holland . . . German fleet surrendered.* After that there was just something about national incomes.

Even before I could read much of this, I could follow it on the maps, because the atlas had special maps for each of the campaigns. And from the map of the Russian front, with its red and black barred and dotted lines, I began to take stock of Russia on the maps of Europe, and the enormous area coloured ochre for Russian slavs on the ethnic map. 'The People's Atlas' gave a lot of stress to trade and national wealth, and set these things out in easy diagrams that a boy could understand. There were yellow blocks to show wealth per head for the various nations: the British one was easily the longest. A row of red and blue freighters showed the size of the world's merchant fleets. Britain's freighter was overwhelmingly the biggest (the figures were for 1914: in 1919 it was all quite different, but they kept pretty quiet about that). A vignette of a harbour showed the world's ports. For all the British and Empire ports the sky was tinted red (sunset colours maybe): the red result was less dumbfounding than the British Empire looked in the world map on Mercator's projection; but not much. The map of 'Colonial powers in 1919' was on Mercator too. Russia was an inconspicuous pale cream, and did not figure in the interesting diagrams underneath, which showed the populations and areas of the 'World's Empires' in proportion to their respective home countries. The biggest home population was China, represented by an ineffective bearded mandarin with what I thought was a fly-swat. On one side of him, but much smaller, was the U.S.A.—represented in lively style as a cowboy. The Frenchman had a straw hat. On the other side, occupying the first place, was a modest-sized English gentleman—an immaculate and incorrigibly dignified figure with top-hat, white waistcoat, stick—and one hand in his pocket. Beside him stood an immense smiling brown coolie in loin-cloth and turban—and one hand holding a mattock, ready for work. Beside this was a diagram called 'areas of the world's empires'. Again, in the place of honour at the head of the list, was an enormous red square with a minute black British Isles in the middle of it. No wonder we had a school holiday on Empire Day. From somewhere or other, I got the idea of the British ('English' I'd have said then of course) as very advanced and ingenious, able to make other people's railways for them and so forth. But also, somewhat to my surprise now, I recall very clearly that I thought—one day everyone will have learnt to do the things we can do now, and then being so small will begin to count. I pored over the map called (somewhat tendentiously) 'the partition of Russia in Europe': but never mind about partitions, Russia was big, you only had to look. I knew it was cold in the far north—places like Greenland and Antarctica didn't stand a chance, though they fascinated me—but I didn't know about continental climates; so Russia's bigness wasn't affected by that. The map of Asia was not done on Mercator's projection. Hence (again rather tendentiously) it made 'British India' look very big and Siberia surprisingly small. All the same, it was still surprisingly big, and this time bright green: the self-effacing cream being reserved for China, which the projection now brought out the size of. But Siberia: *Ob* . . . *Yenisei* . . . *Lena* . . . I was seven or eight when I spelt out those rivers. Nobody could tell me anything about them, but the map showed they were enormous. And there were people there too—towns, even far up north. The map showed them, right up above the Arctic Circle. When I learnt that Siberia was bitterly cold, it occupied my thoughts all the more.

*Chapter seven*

# The monstrous regiment of women

Women's gossiping voices come back to me clearly from childhood. They used to be very loud and regular—almost mechanical; and extraordinarily vehement, though quite without expression. Mrs. Figg at No. 4 Lonsdale Road and Mrs. Freshwater at No. 10, used to converse across the intervening silence of 6 and 8. Their 'clack', as my mother scornfully called it,, was easy to hear even inside our house which was No. 6 in the road that ran at right angles. These two were by far the best clackers in the neighbourhood, and Mrs. Figg was the best of all. She was in the top class, and could rattle on at top speed for a long time at a stretch. No one could break in. She waved and contorted her hands all the while, twisted her body about, nodded and shook her head, and never once made a break in her clatter.

My mother was a good mimic. She could do Mrs. Figg talking to the runner-up Mrs. Freshwater, and she took first one part, then the other. It was all the better for being in dumb-show. You heard the two voices alternating, simply from how my mother imitated their other tricks. She said I used to go purple in the face with laughing at her antics when she was in this mood. Certainly I used to be unable to breathe, and she had to thump my back for me.

I find it hard to remember my father laughing, though he had a good sense of humour. He was one of those men who take part in fun and simple gaiety with a kind of glazed, droll expression. His eyes would open wide, and his mouth would open too in a broad fixed grin with a little twist to it. He enjoyed a joke all right. Sometimes he chuckled, and he would put in curt sarcastic comments of his own. 'Cats!' he would utter with scornful intensity, or 'screaming bitches!' His face didn't change, but he put great force into his words, and we laughed all the more. 'Screaming bitches!' was also what he usually said when he found a soprano singing as he searched for stations on the 'wireless'. He was quick to turn the knob further on.

My father was in some ways a man of insight and judgement; but not consciously, he didn't know about words like that, and I am afraid my mother always insisted on her own superiority of mind, and convinced him too. Yet it was he who used to shout, 'It's the *principle* of the thing!' when they had a dispute, and the true pearls of wisdom which came my way were all his. Almost, he thought in proverbs. He was even unsophisticated, unspoiled enough to be able to create them. 'There's a right way, and a best way' he once blurted out, when we were putting some toy model together, and I said he wasn't doing it the way it said in the box. 'There's excuses and fucking excuses!' he once retorted to my mother furiously when she was trying to defend someone. I still think that's true.

This in my father shaded off into something which had the simplicity but lacked the insight. Once we went for a bicycle-ride. I had a new bicycle: he happened to be in his best clothes (a navy-blue suit). We went down Crown Ash hill at Biggin: one in four-and-a-half, the sign said, on an unmetalled lane. I put my back brake on—but I remembered that if you put your front brake on hard, you pitch over the handlebars. Everyone had warned me. So I left it off. So I gained speed; though not, I thought, enough to matter. But he must have released his brake when he saw me go ahead; he came rattling downhill, caught me up, grabbed my shoulder, slowed me down, and in a trice had us both in the hedge. 'You silly young fool,' he blazed at me: 'you might have broken your neck and *Torn My Trousers*!' There was no question of a sly joke. My mother was inclined to be indignant about this ascending order of importance when I told her, but all the same we had more laughter until I couldn't breathe and she went rosy pink with her eyes watering. Heaven, how we laughed in those days! We must have been hungry for gaiety, all three of us.

Jokes like this lasted us for years. We came back to them again and again. We could throw our meal-times into fits of laughter simply by uttering one of the stock family jokes somehow *à propos*. My mother, especially, had a keen sense of the ridiculous; and in a society precariously near the lower edge of respectability, always aware of that, always making efforts not to fall, she was surrounded by it. Mrs. Taylor delighted her for months, and through her me, because when her husband (who was a clerk in a solicitor's office) got promotion enough to go to work in a bowler, black jacket, and striped trousers, she waved at his retreating figure, and proudly announced to us, from her front garden gate, 'professional man!' So, with her usual display of nods, waves, bows and mock pomposity, my mother used to do Mr. Taylor going off in the morning as a 'professional man'. Another phrase she had a special turn with was 'I'm given to understand. . . .' Some local husband, I forget which, used this about his being the father of one of his children—not as a joke, but as a suitably dignified and formal expression of the facts of the case. Another phrase which tickled her, and with which she tickled us, was the veiled threat, 'put 'im down at Croydon'. This meant, to issue a summons against someone. 'Drag 'im through the courts' was also something I heard spoken in all seriousness as a child, though I now find that hard to believe: but most of the adults I knew were wholly unselfconscious. Nothing in their lives could have rendered them otherwise. They did not read the novels in which their kind was satirized (let alone have the capacity to apply satire to themselves); and the satirical portraiture of radio and television had of course not begun.

My mother used also to see the funny side of our next-door neighbour, Mr. Meadows. Mr. Meadows was a piano-tuner. He and his wife belonged—just—to the more established middle-class families of the street. They conversed occasionally with my parents (or at least my mother) over the garden fence, but they kept their distance a little, as I was aware even then. Mr. Meadows, a mild but gloomy man, was given to lugubrious inanities like 'if things don't clear up, Madge, we shall have to see'. Once, dropping her voice, 'Madge' confided to my mother that Mr. Meadows had said he 'felt like ending it all', and had thought about one of the beams in the veranda. No doubt my mother was right not to take this with the slightest seriousness, but I should think Mr. Meadows was genuinely a depressed man. He had big drooping whiskers, and looked like a witless version of Thomas Hardy. His daughter Polly was learning the piano, and for some years we heard her tinkling, to no very good purpose, on the other side of the wall. But in the end, I believe, she became proficient, and earned her living as a music teacher. She was a mild, shy girl who had long straight hair, light brown, and a long neck. Modestly, she used to keep her head bowed. I have since wondered if she was beautiful, just a little.

There was absolutely nothing malicious in how my mother mimicked the neighbours. I never knew her say or do a malicious thing in her life. She simply had a good sense of humour, a lot of fun, and a talent for imitation. She did not see that she herself, and what she said and what she cared about, were open to the same treatment; but although she would have been a different person if she could have seen this in a funda-mental way, within limits she could laugh at herself—she sometimes used to go pink with indignation and merriment combined, if ever I tried to turn the tables on her, and occasionally she would guy herself. Sometimes, if she had been going for me over something, and then had to go away to attend to work in the house, she would come back with a solemn air, and put one foot forward and the tip of her straightened forefinger on the top of the table while the rest of her hand was closed. Then she would say, as if it were the end of the world, 'Take . . . These . . . Instructions.' I used to have fits of choked laughter, mixed with fear, waiting for this ridiculous performance to begin; but when I was a big boy I once recalled it to her memory, teasing her about it; and she quite convinced me that it was partly a sort of game for her.

Another similar trick of hers was, from time to time, to forbid me to engage in whatever activities were in question '. . . of any kind, sort, type, description . . . *or variety*'. This was another respect, a small one, in which you can see how anything to do with legality and the law had a mystery and a magic for people like us. I can vividly remember how her face lit up with astonishment, fury and amusement when at the age I think of seven or eight, in the middle of one of our rows, I began to mimic her—striking a ham-actor attitude and mouthing 'do *What* you're told, *When* you're told, *What* you're told, *When* you're told.' I must come back to the rows we had in our family. In some ways I must have been a difficult child, though not really in the gallows bracket.

Although my mother laughed at gossiping, she enjoyed a gossip well enough herself. Sometimes she got drawn into Mrs. Figg's orbit: but I think she found that overpowering. Her closest friend was Mrs. Crabb at No. 12. Mrs. Crabb was a dark woman, not altogether unlike my mother to look at, though with a round face and features. I think that as a girl she may have been quite attractive in a plump sort of way. I can't remember if she had been a nurse in her young days, or a wardmaid. My mother used to talk to me about being a wardmaid. I gathered that this was a walk of life low beyond words, given over to floor-scrubbing and emptying of bedpans.

Mrs. Crabb was a good-hearted, simple woman my mother was really fond of; though (rightly I suspect) she thought her rather silly sometimes. 'O my godfather's dick!' was Mrs. Crabb's favourite ejaculation. She used it on all sorts of occasions to vent her astonishment or distress—she was a distressful woman—but seemed not to understand its meaning, for otherwise she was modest-spoken and respectable. 'When I'm gone, they'll know', she used to end long disquisitions on the troubles to which she was put by her family.

Mrs. Crabb's husband worked at a large multiple store in Croydon. He worked 'in the wood-working line', and sometimes, I think, as what my mother called a 'shop-walker': the kind of assistant who tells you which counter to go to in a big store, and generally keeps an eye on things. This was of course much above what my mother had another of her vivid words for, a mere 'counter-jumper'. I do not hear English used now with the colour and force of how she used it. Recently one of my colleagues, a most distinguished man in his own line, was confiding in me about someone else, and said, 'When a man does a thing like that, he's a *bastard*, you just know he's a *bastard*'—Almost for the first time in years, I heard English with the old blunt finality, and silently saluted a background like my own. Not, of course, that that was a term we could ever have used of anyone to their face, however lightly and in joke. Nor was it part of my mother's vocabulary. In any case, she always reacted more sharply to folly than to vice: she met it more often. I can recall the concentrated fury and disgust in her voice when she passed judgement on someone in the worst terms she knew: 'the . . . *jackanapes*!!' That meant the ultimate in grotesque irredeemable folly.

For most of my time at Waverley Road, Mrs. Crabb had only one child, a boy called Charlie who was almost exactly my own age. He was my closest friend, and in fact my only close friend, during this time: a heavily-built, plumpish boy—I could run much the faster. Once, when our mothers were busy together at their gossip which to us had no end, he and I went through a gap in the fence at the end of whatever road it was, and explored a plot of waste-ground until an angry brown dog chased us, and we took to our heels. I was far ahead by the time we got to the fence; and as Charlie came through, the dog bit his bottom—not badly, but enough to tear his trousers and cause his mother much distress and some indignation, not very reasonably, at my expense. She was an affectionate mother. 'Oh, the little angel-face!' she once exclaimed, in her distressful tones, as she flew to the rescue of her son who had fallen down or something. But it was an improvement on the truth.

The Crabb household was a much more middle-class one than ours, and had a print of *The Boyhood of Raleigh* on the wall. They also had a parrot. It was grey and red, a fine bird, and sometimes the feathers of its big crest shot suddenly forwards and upwards. But this was a rare treat. Charlie also used to have ambitious Christmas parties. Once there was a sort of booth like a Punch-and-Judy show, fitted out with curtains; and at a certain stage in the party, we all had to find a chair in front of it, the gas was turned out, the curtains were drawn—and there, in a small but wholly strange, brightly lit world, a stranger, who looked a little like one of the characters in Charlie's weekly 'comic', sang a funny song, and announced himself as Mr. Peppercorn. 'No, it's Mr. Crabb!' I blurted out from the darkness. I was probably five and a half at the time, and sound like an odious child: but I think the facts were not like that. There must have been six or eight children in the room, and quite possibly none of us had so much as heard of theatres. I remember the bright colours of this sudden apparition, and how I really wondered, for the first line or so of the comic song, whether this were a miraculous other-world: as if Father Christmas were real after all (I'd recently learned he wasn't), or the Crabbs had paid the real Mr. Peppercorn to come down from the printing works in London. It was a genuine discovery that I blurted out: up to then I had never encountered dramatic illusion or the convention we observe about it. For a few seconds I had responded not to the mere magic of the theatre, but to magic of a realler kind—the thing itself. It has not often come my way since.

After my mother and father, I suppose that the people I knew best during my childhood were the two old ladies who lodged with us, and whose being in the house meant that so far as I was concerned it was a very small house, with just a kitchen, scullery, and two bedrooms.

Miss Chasteney was a congenial lodger for my mother, because in her younger days she had been a music teacher. Now she played no more, because her fingers had rheumatism; but she revered Chopin and Liszt, and could concur knowingly over the difficult passages. I think also she had once sung in a choir, and knew Stainer's Crucifixion. She spoke in a musical, tired, refined voice—its refinement also made my mother glad to have her, and we thought of her as a person of some superiority and even authority.

When I was very young she had still gone out quite often, and I think still given a few lessons. Later she kept largely to her room, and later still to her bed. She was a small, dainty, fragile woman, with tidy grey hair. In the house, it was usually crimped into curlers all over her head. She wore grey, and mauve, and when she went out, a trim little hat with a veil, and a black ribbon in a bow in front. She was always in a shawl, and she had several, big handknitted ones in grey or mauve or cream. And a black one. She used to read to me with dignity and patience and something like remote kindliness.

This was in the larger of the two back bedrooms; which was her room, where she kept a bright little fire with buckets of coal that we used to lug upstairs for her. Towards the end, I was big enough to do this once or twice myself. I think she was a very clean woman. Her smell was of washed wool, and of old clothes kept fresh, and sometimes of lavender. In my early childhood she used to slip unostentatiously through our kitchen to the outside lavatory. Later on, she had to have a commode in her bedroom. She ailed very slowly, of old age and rheumatoid arthritis. In the end she got pneumonia, and went to the 'infirmary' (work'us, that is), where she died in her early seventies, when I was about six and a half.

Miss Chasteney knew two people besides ourselves. One was Mr. Waldron, the blind piano-tuner, who used to go up for a chat with her when he came to tune my mother's piano. He was a man in late middle age, with a plump face, but grey and lined, who lived—I think by himself—somewhere over Penge way. To call on him and ask him to come (having a standing arrangement would not have been our way) we had to go through the allotments into Love Lane, and then turn left between the big hawthorn hedges until we got to a major landmark in my childhood terrain: the dark footway tunnel, long and low and narrow, that ran in grey brick under the disused railway-line. This was the only point at which I could cross that line (or so it seemed, because at the only other point, the Goat House Bridge, all the lines were together, so you didn't notice). Beyond it lay what seemed another world, centred on Marlow Road, which was very long, almost perfectly straight, fairly wide, and broken up at regular intervals by side-roads.

It was often quite foggy in London when I was a child, and Marlow was one of the roads you could not see to the end of if there was only a little fog, and had to keep on down, for a long time, just walking blind, if there was much. Sometimes it was thick enough for the far side of the road to disappear. Another time, my mother came home up it alone after dark, and it was so thick that she had to touch the garden fences all the way along. At the bottom, in the main road, there were a few shops, but never many people. Anyway, it was down there that Mr. Waldron lived. If it was foggy up Marlow Road when he came to see us, that made no difference to him.

Mr. Waldron was just an acquaintance of Miss Chasteney's; but she also had someone whom we knew as her nephew. Certainly he looked like her: or rather (for he was years younger) he looked remarkably like a picture of her taken many years ago. His name was Willie Tressider. Willie was a short, lightly-built man, with delicate, shapely hands smaller than my mother's, an olive complexion, dark eyes, a shapely longish nose, and black wavy hair. He might have been Spanish, but he struck one as a little dandified or even effeminate. He wore a black jacket and black striped trousers like a clerk in those days. Usually he had stiff cuffs with what looked like gold cuff-links, and a wing collar with a tie-pin in his dark tie. He also had, as then was not uncommon, a monocle on a black ribbon. He lodged somewhere up the hill, but was constantly in our house, either coming to see Miss Chasteney (who did his needlework for him among other things: but he was genuinely attentive and obliging to her in return), or turning the music for my mother with his beautifully manicured hands (they had black hairs, thick, on the backs), or singing in his mannered but by no means untrained tenor voice. He had a light voice, quite a good one, but sang after the style of a concert artist: as fruitily as he could, and with much drama and *rubato*. His preference was for songs of a powerfully masculine kind. 'Captain John Macpherson', about a skipper whose dearest love was the long, lonely and hazardous voyage, is what I recall best. When I was a young man, and had a little of my mother's talent for mimicry, I used to render the chorus of this ballad in the Tressider style—O. . . .h!—*Some* go *here*, *some* go *there*! and so on—and make her laugh, as she so often had me.

Willie Tressider also played the piano; but his playing exercised my mother's mind a good deal. As a singer he could accompany himself nimbly and gracefully, with plenty of fingers dancing up from the keyboard, and head becking down at it, and black curls falling over his brows, and all the other pianist's tricks. Sometimes he played from music. But here my mother reserved her judgement. He never sight-read. In fact, he firmly refused to play anything from music except certain pieces which he knew really well; and with these, my mother noticed that he adapted them a good deal to his own style, changing the hard bits and turning the page rather as he liked. So she concluded that he more or less played these pieces by ear as well. I think that once, through the window, she had seen him sitting at our kitchen *table* (which stood just beside the piano), waving his arms and strumming on the table-top, grimacing with his face and waving his head about, and engaged in an intense *sotto voce* tra-la-la which made her think that in imagination he was thundering out the most difficult of Liszt's Rhapsodies before a large and enraptured audience.

Certainly in the street (although he used always to walk with a swift and dapper tread as though time were short and others were expecting him), I used to see him talking vigorously to himself as he went along; and once or twice my mother and I saw him, in the distance, slow down until he stood still for a moment, in vehement shadow talk, before he went on. And perhaps the general pattern of his life had something of this too. From time to time he told us that he was to sing in some suburban ballad-concert. Probably he did. But often and often he would give an important-seeming glance at his big gold pocket-watch (Miss Chasteney had given him this), and say goodbye, telling us he had an appointment, but not telling us what it was. 'Professional', he would say with a wave of the hand and a pre-occupied air; and off he would go. Occasionally he would begin a talk, in a man-to-man way, with my father; but my father it was who saw him, shortly after he had left for one of those mysterious appointments, at a loose end in the street in quite the wrong direction. From time to time he took a job, as a clerk or something of the sort; and we would hear quite a lot about this. Then we would hear no more. All in all we thought that, apart from singing sometimes, he had no work at all. We didn't understand the true facts of such a life in the England of the 1920s, any more (though we liked him and were kind enough) than we responded as I should wish to, now, to his lonely dramatization and elaborate façade. We thought, really, that Miss Chasteney kept him. We also thought that he might be her son.

Many years later, I encountered someone else whose fantasy life was if anything more extreme. Coming home from London on a rush-hour train, I sat next to a middle-aged man in a mackintosh. With a great air of concentration he wrote all the time in an exercise book. Over and over, he hesitated, seeming deep in thought, pen poised—then dashed down a line, then pondered again. The pattern on the page of what he wrote made it look like elaborate mathematical equations. But I was a little surprised, though much impressed, that someone should be able to transform such intricate equations at such speed, page after page, and without ever a long pause or a single erasure. In the end, from the corner of my eye, I studied what he wrote quite closely. Possibly, I suppose, there might be a mathematician on a suburban rush-hour train, doing such advanced work that I could not distinguish a single symbol he used, nor a single one of the operations he carried out. But I think that, for the whole half-hour, what that man did was to set down a wholly meaningless scribble, meant to look like abstruse mathematics and impress those who watched him.

We had two lodgers in the house: Miss Chasteney in the back bedroom upstairs, and Miss Chapman, an elderly acquaintance of the Meadowses, in the 'parlour' at the front downstairs. She was a plump old woman, with a round wrinkled face and straight white hair that she did in a bun. She always wore an ankle-length black frock with a dark grey apron over it. I think that in the past she had been in service with the Meadows' family. When she went out, which she almost never did, she wore a black bonnet. She didn't play with me, nor read to me, but quite often I was allowed to go into her room and play by myself, quietly, on the floor, or sit in the chair opposite her and look at a book. A few times she had me watch her while she played patience. There seemed always to be a fire in her room, but it was always a low one. It was a dull red, or almost black, and never made a sound.

There was a lot of furniture in the room, old and dark all of it; and heavy curtains, with more curtains, these ones made of net, across the windows. So the room, which faced north, was always half dark, and the air quiet and still.

Time seemed to pass slowly there. Miss Chapman had an elderly silent parrot, green all over, who let me scratch his head. Very occasionally he let out a low croaking sound as I did it. Towards four o'clock Miss Chapman used to put her small sooty kettle on the trivet, and it warmed slowly, singing a mournful little waver of a tune. She would give me a cup of tea, and usually, out of a big biscuit-tin in the cupboard by her chair, a piece of seed-cake. I loved seed-cake. It was with her I found out that when people get up, they leave the seat of their chair warm. Hers used to be very warm. I also discovered that if I listened carefully, I could hear her stomach rumbling and gurgling all the time. She was an old woman, well over seventy. She paid us half-a-crown a week.

For a few months, when I was really small, my mother had a charwoman once a week, and a half-crown was also her wages for four hours' work in the morning. Her name was Mrs. Pie, and she came from one of the cottages in Love Lane. She was a skinny, scrawny woman, with lean muscles on her long arms and legs, and a brown wrinkled skin. She had very dark eyes that stared a little, a gold tooth, moles on her face, and feet like boats. To work in, she wore a faded green apron and tied her hair up in a rag. From half past seven she used to work at the house next door, No. 8, most mornings of the week; and quite often I was woken up by a continuous bumping, rattling sound, that seemed to move steadily down the wall from the upper room to the lower one, and puzzled me a lot. When I asked my mother what it could be, she told me it was Mrs. Pie doing their stairs.

Mrs. Pie was tremendous.

She cleaned our house on Monday mornings while my mother stood at the copper or the sink in the scullery, and did our week's washing. I never saw anything else like it. When she took the dustpan and brush to the banisters of our stairs it was like a gun-fight for minutes on end. When she did out the grate, she fought that too; and that was another noise I remember coming through the wall: Mrs. Pie fighting the grate at No. 8. When 11 o'clock came, my mother and Mrs. Pie used to have a break. My mother made herself some tea, and Mrs. Pie attacked and swiftly defeated the other part of her wages: a quart of stout. It was at this time that she began to clack; and once having started it went on more or less for the rest of the morning. My mother was no bad talker, but with Mrs. Pie she learnt to be a listener. Mrs. Pie flew at conversation as she flew at the stairs or the grate. She would stand up from her work, one boat forward, and lean back with one hand on her broom and one on her hip, and it would pour from her in a cascade. Then at the end—out would come her skinny brown hand for that single coin—half-crowns seemed very big to me in those days, my hand felt heavy if it held one—and she would talk herself out through the door. Sometimes, on the way home from shopping, I remember standing outside the 'Signal' by the railway bridge in Portland Road for a moment or so, while my mother slipped inside to get the quart of stout for Mrs. Pie.

# Chapter eight

# Going into details

My mother and father used to have rows. In her middle years (and no doubt before) my mother had great energy of mind. The plain truth was that she was a woman who should have had an intellectual life, and she had none. She had no access to books, and none to people whose talk was intelligent and educated. From the middle-class country-town respectability of her mother, and her Victorian-schoolmaster, natural-historian father, she had learnt nothing but a bit of snobbery and a love of plants and birds. She had had an altogether exceptional mezzo-soprano voice, and could play the piano excellently. Her love of music was very real. But it was a player's love. She seldom wanted to listen to music unless she had sung in it or played it; and her taste was wholly for the pianistic romantics of the last century. She had never been given the vaguest sense of social problems, or political ones, or the visual arts; and had never been anywhere, and never read anything except a handful of books, mostly trash, that in my childhood she read again and again.

All these things, sorry as they are, I find not to her discredit, but that of others. She was as she was because her childhood and youth had starved and stunted what they should have fed and fostered. She remained with great moral courage, and great dignity of bearing and manner when she chose to assume it ('Coming the duchess' we used to call it: but it commanded genuine respect, it wasn't a silly fake). Besides this, she had a vigorous, penetrating and sensitive mind. She never, never gave up anything through weakness or indifference; but she could genuinely be persuaded, and change her view. She could listen, and could heed, in a way that belongs to the humble and good. In her later middle age, when I was grown up, she would sometimes ask me to find her a book—a classic novel, say—and with diffidence and modesty, and in a language of total unsophistication, would comment on it in terms that showed she had real judgement. Besides these things, she had many other good qualities of mind and personality. Had all gone for her as it might have done, she could have been a notable professional woman or the wife of a distinguished man. That was the quality she had in her innermost self. But all had been left in part to go to waste. Without training and without scope, she had fallen into a life which made no adequate demand on her. Over the years, her gifts ran out on the sand, or were worn away with work, or blazed up and burnt themselves out to no purpose.

This was why my mother and father had rows. I did not see it then, but I see it now. When there was a difference between them, her remarkable mind was brought into play in all its range and depth. My father exasperatedly called it 'going into details'. 'For Chrissake', he would say, 'don't start going into details'. But she always did; her athletic mind knew no other form of exercise. She had a kind of glowing confidence in the power of discussion, analysis and disputation, not only to find the truth but also to leave everyone else convinced of it: it is a confidence that comes only to those who are highly intelligent, and yet wholly unversed in the powers and limits of power which belong to the intelligence. To my father, whom she rightly thought less gifted than herself, she never yielded a point, never modified her position, never let anything go. Even as a child, I began to see how unreasonable her powers to reason could make her. I now know that to let things go, to resign oneself to the ways of others, or to the fact that they will or cannot see the point, must come either from content and fulfilment, or from sophistication and discipline. I think she did not have these.

So she would harangue my father, and analyse and elucidate for his benefit. Of course it did no good. All he could bring on his side was a sense of humour and a bit of countryman's commonsense. 'Here . . . endeth . . . the First Lesson', he would say at the close of a long going-into-details speech; or 'for Which let us be Truly Thankful'. But the fact is, that although she was far more intelligent than he, both of them, on balance, were on the wrong side of that great frontier which divides the species into truly reasonable beings and the majority. He was wholly unreasonable himself. 'So I'm a liar!' he would exclaim (unless in a specially good mood) if what he said were subjected to demur; and she for her part demanded to be accepted as unquestioned arbiter in every question of conduct, because of the allegedly gentlemanly status of her father and gentlewomanly status of her mother. In the clumsy, half-helpless way of a wholly uneducated man, my father would be in the right of it when he rejected this dreamworld of hers with angry if muddled scorn. A mother who had done for her eldest daughter only what my grandmother had done for hers, was to no one's credit; save in fact, as I realized later, as a woman of iron-strong will and beautifully distinguished features. She also had a seventeen-inch waist: the smallest, I believe, in the county. I cannot set a value on this, since I have never got to know a girl who had the same. If your father was a schoolmaster in a primary school in a country town, you can only insist that he was a 'gentleman' in a rather special way. But probably he was in a sense, as a younger son of old Mr.

Astbury. Yet old Mr. Astbury wasn't anything to be over-proud of either. For all his horseriding and good looks, he lost that fine little manor-house in the country.

My mother's mother's family one could indeed think a lot of. Inn-keepers of the coaching inns between Reading and Oxford they were, and masters, one or two of them, of scores and scores of post-horses. Others were country builders. One was a famous master-mason in the seventeenth century: there is still a builder in that branch of the family. Everywhere, going back that side, you come to men renowned for their swimming (or their music with fiddle or country church-organ), and women famous or notorious for their beauty. One, so legend had it, did penance in her nightdress, in Benson churchyard, for the trouble her beauty got her into (and I suppose her night-dress too). Another left the spinster aunts, for three generations, fussing over some vast claim in the Court of Chancery, because she was thought to have got a child from a peer of the realm. Somewhere, way back, comes a Portuguese Sephardim Jew, somewhere else a 'Bedwin' whom my mother had been taught to think, in a puzzled way, was an Arab: but a gipsy he was of course. Colourfulness, zest, strength, beauty, the skill of the craftsmen—these one may indeed be modestly proud of: but my mother's values found no place for them. Once, long after, I had lunch with a great-uncle on this side, in the Angel restaurant in Oxford. We were served by a strapping, bustuous waitress in her early forties. After a while he put down his knife and fork, rested his gaze firmly on her, and said, in a thinking way, 'that's a fine woman'. No one could mistake what was in his mind, and he was seventy-five. My mother, though a little shocked, would have been also tickled as well, if someone had told her that this was the sort of thing to be proud of in one's forbears. She would have seen the point of it. But as it was, her pride went out to other things.

Once a really big row got under way, it would last for a great time—hours and hours, all day, two days, a week once or twice. It ramified back into the past over years, even genera-

tions. It could take in everything and distort and confuse everything. So far as I remember, it seemed to me like madness at
the time; though even for a child, an intriguing and to some
extent obsessive madness. Big family rows can be very stimu-
lating and educative, both intellectually and emotionally, for a
child who hears them through; but I think they rather take it
out of you, and fray the nerves, and stimulus and education are
better arranged otherwise.

Looking back, I feel sorry for my father, because of how
much the cards were stacked against him. Strong and wiry as
he was, he must often have been very very tired. He was
nothing like as clever as my mother, and he had no defence
against her claim to superior understanding because of the
higher level of society—so called—that she came from. He
had no defence because he had absolutely no knowledge of
social or political realities. He indeed had a violent and savage
temper, became ferociously angry, and occasionally threw the
china about; though this was rare. Once or twice my mother
joined in.

His having been gassed in the 1914–18 war also contributed;
but the main thing was that in spite of all the bad parts of his life
he was so often lighthearted and gay. When he got very angry,
true enough, he would do things that from one point of view
were silly. He would announce that he was leaving home and
would thunder out of the house: I can still hear the crash the
front door used to make. But then my mother would take me
up to the front bedroom and we would peep round the net
curtain stretched across the lower halves of the windows, and
watch him march angrily up the slope, past the allotments
towards the pillar-box: his grey trilby hat would be pulled
down low over his eyes, and his hands thrust into the pockets
of his navy-blue overcoat. My mother would be chuckling—it
was unkind of her, but she also had been in the thick of it all—
as we would see his step falter and go slower; and then he
would stop, turn angrily round, come back, fling the door
open with his key, and say 'I've come back for my shirt', or

something of the kind. And then of course everything would begin once more, slowly mounting to a big row again. He looked silly, of course, turning round halfway along the allotments, and more or less the same place each time. But he wasn't laughable: thought about, it was very much not that.

They used to start rows over small things, usually, and make themselves ridiculous if you turn your back on the sadness of it. Once the whole of Christmas Day was made a chaos because my father (who was on holiday that time) washed himself all over in the scullery and then went to put on clean underclothes and couldn't find any. So he got very angry, and my mother didn't smooth him down but the opposite. He angrily insisted that he had an unassailable right to 'Clean Pants on a Christmas Day!' and made my mother burst into ripples of laughter. He couldn't in the least see the funny side, which made it much funnier. But if one shifts one's point of view a little, and remembers the work he did and at the same time what a clean man he was, it didn't have a funny side, but was wretched.

My father was certainly a very clean man. His shirts and underclothes used to get black with the soot and grime of London, because the East End in those days was a black hell, and the inner southern suburbs were quite as dirty as they are today. My mother used to tell me that in those days you could tell at an inquest (she meant the autopsy) if a dead man had been a countryman or a Londoner. His lungs inside would be red, or else they would be black. But my father used to smell of the Lifebuoy or Sunlight soap, red or yellow, that we had in our kitchen. I remember how he washed in the morning (my mother used to take hot water up to the bedroom and wash by herself). He stood at the kitchen sink in his vest, his braces dangling down and his legs wide apart, and filled the big enamel bowl with water from the cold tap. Then he lathered himself ferociously, then he rinsed himself over and over again with water from the cold tap. He turned this on very fast. He never used a face flannel, only his hands, and gasped with shock and joy whenever the cold water splashed him. I used to get sent out if he wanted to wash the lower half of himself, because in those days one never saw one's father naked. I seldom saw him with his vest off, in fact (and I never saw my mother in less than a thick nightgown or her big petticoat and probably her stockings on).

When my father shaved it was quite a ritual. He used an enamel mug and a shaving stick and a safety razor, and it took him a long time. He wouldn't have a cut-throat in the house; and this shows that at bottom he was as sane and shrewd as a crow. He stropped the blade, with almost a dainty movement, on the butt of his hand; and he wielded the razor deliberately, almost daintily, too, making each stroke quite separate from the last, and breathing heavily through his nose, though he opened his mouth wide, and contorted his face into funny grimaces. I used to watch him intently, rather as my daughter now does me (though I don't shave at all his way). If I asked him something, of course it would be in an odd voice that he'd reply because of the face he was pulling so as to get at the whiskers. But he soon got irritable if I pestered him then. Poor man: he so easily turned the joke against himself. 'I wish to *Krod* you'd be quiet!' he once shouted at me (though this wasn't while shaving). This confusing of two Persons of the Trinity was for long a family joke, though my father never found it funny and I am not sure that he saw its point.

## Chapter nine

# Up the garden path

We had a little back-garden which meant a lot to my mother. Much of it was taken up with the chicken sheds and rabbit hutch, and by the chicken shed stood the wireless aerial, made of round metal tubes that screwed together. It made me happy and proud, when I saw that our wireless aerial was the tallest to be seen all round. One of the worst rows my mother and father ever had, started because I found the soil by the wireless mast easy to dig, and began extensive trench warfare operations for my tin soldiers. My father said that this might bring the mast down (I had dugouts in mind, though he didn't know that: so he might have been right). My mother replied that if a small boy digging with an old kitchen knife could endanger the mast, it must be unsafe anyhow. From that they went on, touching on related matters, and recapitulating the main and other points, for several days.

In spite of all the sheds, a certain amount of garden was left, and my mother grew flowers and had a little grass. We had some hollyhocks that grew by the veranda trellis, but otherwise no perennials. Our flowers were annuals—shirley poppies, yellow and orange marigolds, 'French marigolds' (these we also knew as South African poppies), 'Iceland poppies', 'love-in-a-mist', its blue flowers in a maze of frail branching stalks, candytuft, and 'love-lies-bleeding' with flowers like enormous crimson tongues. The seed all came from my grandfather's garden: my mother had got it when she first started her own, and she saved it and re-sowed it each year. Most of these plants she was still growing, from the original stock, when she died many years after the period of this book. The plots of grass were so small that we could clip all of them with the shears. Anyway, we didn't have a mower. I liked gardening, and I used to do this grass myself quite often. My mother still had the old cottage idea that it was nice to have little strips of grass, maybe a foot wide, between the flower borders and the path.

We had a kitchen garden—though if anything it was smaller than the kitchen—where my mother grew things like lettuce, carrots, radishes and spring onions. She liked spring onions a lot, but used to be shy of what they did to her breath. We never grew potatoes. My father dug it over sometimes, and occasionally did other things: but this was intermittent. My mother saw the garden as her exclusive property really. I don't know which of these two facts was cause, and which effect. 'Finished with the bloody garden' he once shouted, after my mother had been into details.

The shed for chickens ran along the whole of the bottom of the garden, and up about half the left-hand side. My father was a good carpenter. Building a shed was easy for him. Just as my mother saw the flowers as hers, so he saw the chickens as his; but from time to time she questioned this on the ground that, as was inevitable of course, she did most of the looking-after, because he was out at work. Really, though neither of them knew, the chicken sheds belonged to me. This was because they were big enough to explore inside: and I had done it.

They were in a number of small bits and pieces, because they had been added to over a longish time. There had to be a section for day-olds, with a lamp to keep them warm, and one for pullets, and one for the broody hens, and one for the laying hens, and one for the cock—and then there were the pigeons. There was a lot to explore inside, and once you had gone in and shut the wire door behind you, you easily got out of sight, and the light was shadowy and you couldn't see the outside world at all. It was also, as a rule, extraordinarily quiet, except for the soft, querulous, rising notes of the hens. They seemed not to think much of my being there, but of course they knew me too well to be really frightened, and I used to move as slowly and quietly as I could. I often spent hours exploring the chicken sheds and turning them, in thought, into better things than they were; and this is why they belonged not to my parents but to me.

On the top of the chicken shed my father built a 'pigeon place', as we called it: we should not have been at ease with a word like pigeon-loft. Part of this was fairly low and ran the whole length of the hen-house; but at the far end was a high part, closed in except for air-vents, where the pigeons roosted and sometimes laid eggs, which meant that I could have a pigeon's egg for my tea. At the other end, nearest to the house, was the pigeon trap. This was another high part: almost a cube, in fact, which seemed to me then to rise to a great height, and be like the tower of a castle. When I saw it again, after a lapse of many years, I was fourteen and it seemed nothing at all. But when I was a little boy, it soared into the sky.

The pigeon-trap was all open, with wire-netting of the largest mesh that would keep the birds in; so I suppose a new pigeon might think there was no barrier at all. My father knocked up some boards to make a platform inside the cage, and it ran along at the same height as the middle part of the roof. Between the roof and the platform ran the mouth of the trap. This was made of a row of stiff pieces of wire, bent in the shape of a U. Each of these was suspended, up-side-down, by two staples. They swung quite free in an inwards direction, but came up against a piece of wood which stopped them from swinging outwards.

As soon as a stray pigeon appeared on a nearby rooftop, my father would go down the garden and sprinkle corn on the pigeon house roof, and the platform inside the cage. Then he would go into the chicken shed, make his way up to the pigeon-place, and let one of the birds out into the cage. If he thought the stray was a hen, he used to let Black Tom out; and we had a hen we called Biddy, that he liked to let through if he thought the stray was a cock.

The captive bird ate the corn inside the trap, on the platform. Sometimes almost at once, sometimes only after a long time and many shifts from housetop to housetop, and then the roof of the cage, and the other end of the hen-shed, the stray bird would come down and down until it began to eat the corn outside the trap. The bird inside, also eating its corn, would coo to it and pout and bow. My father always put much more corn inside the trap than outside. Sooner or later—though often after many many cranings of its neck through the wires, while all three of us stood at a window and never took our eyes off it—the stray bird would go through the trap and eat the other corn. Then my father would go into the cage himself, take the bird in his hands (he could do this very deftly) and put it through into the dark part. I think that then some time later he went again and 'handled' it. The birds became tame very quickly... My mother could make delicious pigeon pies, and I got especially to enjoy the hearts. Black Tom, who would sit on my parents' fingers and eat the corn they held in their hands, did not have his neck wrung until he was very very old, and rather tough. It was quite a special Sunday when we ate him, and I think we had mixed feelings about it. He had got us so many birds. Biddy's turn came later, but she was only a hen.

These birds were often ringed, and our own birds were

ringed too, I think; they were our property, needless to say. Once we caught a racing pigeon—or so we called it, and it was indeed a slim, sleek, elegant bird. But after twenty-four hours we released it, and it flew away all pink and brown, and very swiftly. My parents had words over this bird, for my father's cupidity and my mother's sense of—or fear of—the law, made it that they could not both see the thing in the same way.

We used to let our own pigeons fly outside: especially on a Sunday when my father was at home. They flew in a closely bunched group in circles, and seldom went out of sight. Pigeons fly high and fast, and bank steeply, and to look at them, you would think that being able to fly made them very happy.

My father was too restless a man to make the ideal gardener; and he wanted to be out in the country. He really used to want that badly. When he learnt about my mother's nest-egg —she kept the knowledge of it from him for a long time, knowing that a wife's possessions were in those days her husband's by law—he used to urge and wheedle her to buy this or that, but above all to buy a motor-bicycle-and-sidecar so that we could get right out of London on it. 'Motor-bike, matey?' he used to say in his most winning tones. He had a lot of charm and amiability when he was happy. So in the end we had an Ariel motor-cycle combination. We didn't have any-where to keep it, so it had to stay in a garage a good ten minutes' walk away.

We had a lot of trouble with that garage. I think they soon realized that my father was feckless with money (he'd never had any, to learn) and my mother, in the background, not feckless but inexperienced and quite unbusinesslike. As I heard about it at the time, they sent in bills which we had already paid, and since of course we hadn't kept the receipts (we didn't, needless to say, pay by cheque, though my mother had that deposit account), we were dunned for it again. This was our version anyhow. Then we agreed to pay the debt off by instalments: but as fast as we caught up on the past, we had new bills to meet for more garaging of the wretched Ariel, and of course all the garaging bills (quarter by quarter or whatever it was) were for one and the same sum, which added to our confusion. I think that in the end my mother took over all the receipts and kept them in her tin, and there came a point when the garage tried their bill-sending once too often, and my mother went along herself, with the tin (I mean the tin box), and really went into details with the manager. And that was that. But it didn't make up for the months of wretchedness and misery, of squabbling among ourselves and worrying over money with a quite new degree of urgency, that came to us from that bike. Not that we didn't, quite often, get worried about the grocer's bill, or milk, or papers or something like that; but those people were obliging and patient, or at the worst a little irritated if you were really a long time. It was only over the motor-bike that we got filled with a sense of being led deeper into difficulties, hectored and then spoken fair, shilly-shallied with over receipts, all the rest of it; and in part it was thinking over those years, when I was a big boy, that made me conscious of how often the little people of the world are tricked and kicked by those who are just above them, and exploit the fact that they write on headed notepaper or sit at desks or have another kind of voice or whatever it may be. I thought I saw how this goes back to teaching children the *what*-you're-told-*when*-you're-told philosophy. You have to learn a bit of *not-bloody-likely* philosophy as well; and since this isn't part of the curriculum anywhere, you have to teach it to yourself. You lose something by acquiring it, but you gain more; and you also frequently have the satisfaction of watching a little jerk run across the faces of people who are trying it on, as they realize that here's one it's not going to work with. You like that, and you need it, if you once saw your parents getting the other thing.

But there was also quite another side to having that motor-bike, because it took us for picnics. We used to go to Caterham (you could do this by bus, but changing twice, and that in the middle of Croydon), and here we could go up on the Downs and pick basinful after basinful of blackberries, which my mother made into splendid puddings. Right on the top of the Downs were two great red-brick walls, built in a circle fifteen feet across maybe, and much higher than a man's head. My parents explained how inside were the vent-shafts for the long long tunnel that runs underneath the Downs. Sometimes as we stood near those walls we could hear the roar of the train, deep underground, seeming immensely remote.

Another place we went to was called Fairchilds, with woods and chalk meadows, and a great many flowers to pick. I found this again for myself, years later, but I never seemed to find the corners I remembered best. When we went to Fairchilds, it seemed as if the motor-bike went dug-dug-dug-dug-dug for miles through little country lanes, and the banks were starred all the way with big white flowers that seemed to freshen and scent the air. When I was seven and saw such things for the first time it seemed an extraordinary, an earthly-paradise drive. Years later I found when I re-visited the place that the lanes just had greater stitchwort along them. But that flower has two existences for me: its modest, familiar self as I see it now, and the great dew-fresh white stars that spattered those green wooded lanes. It was the same with the bluebells in Spring Park Woods, which we used also to ride out to. They made a blue carpet over the glades: nowadays bluebells cannot really be the same, or at least I only know one place where they are, and I'm not telling where that is.

This was all we did with our motor-bike. My father never used it to go work, and the one big excursion we used to make, we did by train. We almost never went to London. By the time I was nine I had been to the Tower and the Zoo, and some people outside our normal circle had taken me to a big London Circus. I had been to the Natural History Museum in South Kensington; and also the Science Museum with a party from my second school. But since we turned the handles provided so that the public could turn them, and the model trains, ships and so on, actually work, not sit silent like boys in a class-room, we were rushed back to school in disgrace, and the headmaster spent the afternoon at his favourite form of physical exercise. My father took me a few times to see matches at the Crystal Palace Football Ground (I was rather frightened of the big crowds going in and coming out, but it was exhilarating too); and sometimes we went to the Crystal Palace, up the very steep hill that only trams could climb, no buses, and the trams only just. There were fine firework displays at the 'Palace', and they used to play the great fountains at the same time.

But for the big excursion we used to go on the Southern Railway to London Bridge, which we walked over to catch the Inner Circle to Paddington; and then one of those big Great Western steam-engines, all shiny green and polished brass, used to rush us smoothly to Reading, saying 'a present for *me*, a present for *me*!' as the bogies clicked over the rails. At Reading we took a middle-sized stopping train for Cholsey, and the West-country burr would begin in the porters' voices. Then from Cholsey we travelled to Wallingford on the branch train pulled by a real puffing Billy; like a toy engine, and pulling one big coach where everybody seemed to know everybody, and they would wave at each other and talk *Wa'unvurd*.

While my grandfather had been headmaster, my grand-parents had lived in a sizeable semi-detached villa with a long garden that ran down to the water-meadow. But when he retired they moved to a red-brick council house beyond the station and minuscule gasometer (the town's only one), and on the way to the Infirmary (i.e. 'work'us', as my mother called it, remembering the pronunciation she had heard from the labourers as a child). My earliest recollection, after that bright fire, is being taken to see my grandfather in the main bed-room of this house, where he was lying ill. The doors in that house all had latches. So we unlatched the bedroom door and went in, and his tired, refined voice said 'hullo John' from out of his beard. This must have been very shortly before he died, which was when I was just over two years old.

That little house was in a bleak place: just a great open field behind, and another in front which rose slightly to some big elm trees (in my mother's childhood they had called that rise the 'Blue Mountains', but she didn't know why). There was a little chintzy parlour where my aunt had her piano, and a living-room with a kitchen range where they kept a low fire, and the lavatory, with a bath room this time, very cold and fresh and country-smelling, outside the back door. There was always a sound of wind in that house: it sighed and blew in soft hollow whistles all day long. Otherwise it was a very quiet house, so I used to listen to the rise and fall of the wind for a long time at a stretch.

There was no hurry in Wallingford. We would go for a walk down towards the town, and many people would recognize my mother and stop and chat leisurely. Once we met my mother's cousin Howard with his brown-owl on his shoulder; and in those days, if you leant over Wallingford Bridge for only five minutes, the chance was you would see a kingfisher. Usually we went to call on my great-aunt Mary. Her house was very very cold, and the sunny front parlour would be dark, with blinds down and curtains drawn. We never went in the sunny room except once for a minute, looking for a paper. Aunt Mary's hands were just twisted white knobs, they were so arthritic. Her brother, the musician who still had so much joy in life at seventy-five, lived in the house too and seemed never to take off his overcoat. If there was a fire in the grate, it would somehow survive on one single coal. Yet it was Aunt Mary who knew more than anyone of the treasure waiting for us in Chancery; treasure to which we had a claim through a Willis who had seen life in other terms than hers; and who linked us by her misdeeds (we were assured), with a belted earl, and through him, back over the centuries, with crowned heads and in the end with the House of Pippin and the Emperor Charlemagne.

Aunt Mary's house, like my grandmother's, was very quiet, and you noticed it in the breaks of her talk. But there was no sound of wind: year after year, the air was still and it was stuffy too.

# Chapter ten

# To the south

One of the less good things about growing up as I did (or others more so of course), is that one gives too much interest and energy to what barely deserves them. I used to spend hours poring over a little brass thing, less than an inch across, which was exactly like a top hat, save that it had a small hole in the centre of what, had it been a top hat, would have been the crown. I think it may have been some fixture for a curtain-rod: but no one in the house could tell me what it was, so for a long time I used to try it on my finger, looking to see how much it really was like a top hat, and puzzling about what it might have been made for. I was deeply interested when I discovered that ordinary safety-pins can be opened on either the one side or the other, and therefore that you can make the point describe an endless course in the air—in one side, up to the top, out the other side, back over the top again, down to the first side, and into the shield once more. I used to stare at the frosted glass of the front door, trying endlessly to find two of the little lop-sided cut figures in it that were exactly the same size and shape. I studied and grew familiar with the different creak of each tread in the flight of stairs. I could tell you which of the stair-banisters were spaced a fraction wider or narrower than the others. In the same way I spent hours over the Virginia creeper that climbed the veranda trellis, seeing how the leaves differed one from another, trying to find exact matches, all the rest of it. I studied the wallpapers endlessly, and slowly, slowly, as my childhood passed, discovered first that there were repeats in the pattern, and then, at last, that the whole room was one great repeat, an endless hushed-up monotony. In the dark, I watched the light made by the vehicle-lamps through a crack in the curtains. This light moves across the ceiling, in a sort of slow blink, in the opposite direction to whatever is going by. I tried hard enough, but I am not sure if I ever saw clearly why this was. There were a lot of other trivial things that had a large place in my thoughts. To some extent, there is no harm in that: childhood is long, there is time to spare, and the mind can find its nourishment in many things. But this makes no difference to the basic fact: that it is wasteful to give good attention to mediocre things.

In this context, it may seem lugubrious, even grotesque, that the two open spaces I remember best from my childhood should be a sewage farm and a cemetery. But it by no means seems like that to me. The cemetery (it was the Crystal Palace District Cemetery, though I had no idea of that name) was fairly new. When I was a small boy, only about one-fifth of it was built up (if I may so put it), and even there, the parts near the two little burial chapels were laid out rather like a park. Moreover, this was all in the far corner from where we came in. On our side, at the end of Harrington Road, there was a trim little red brick lodge, and then a fine curving avenue of horse-chestnuts, half white and half crimson. When they were in flower they were really marvellous. I learnt that the white ones were called Candles, and that the red ones came from India (with which in general we linked colourful and exotic-looking things). Beneath the chestnut trees grew a specially fine, soft, silky grass: we found this grass nowhere else, and called it 'cemetery grass'. Stroking it, and touching my face against it, was one of my earliest sensuous pleasures, strong enough for me to recall the sensation still.

In this part of the cemetery, the grass was left uncut; and to right and left of the entrance drive it made two big meadows, the left running gently up to the disused railway-line, and the right sloping gently down to the line of big poplars that bordered the cemetery and the sewage farm. All this was simply mown for hay once or twice a year. Before it was cut, the grass grew so tall that at the beginning of my childhood it came above my head, and for years it seemed easy to hide from my mother, even if she were quite near, by lying down. (I don't know if it was.) And she could hide from me. It was thick with flowers too: sometimes the bottom end would be almost solid with the gold of buttercups; and there were blue flowers, and moon-daisies; and plenty of cuckoo-flowers or ladies'-smocks, in the wetter parts down near the poplars. We picked such big bunches of flowers that they sometimes seemed thicker than my waist, and were so heavy to carry that I got really tired. I think there are far fewer flowers in the fields now than there used to be. And alongside the chestnuts were avenues of fir trees: the ground was a deep carpet of pine-needles, and we could collect baskets of the hard, dry cones, almost black. They opened to a prickliness as they dried.

We seldom spent much time in the built-up part of the cemetery, but there was one grave I went through to several times. In the eastern corner where the graves had only just begun to appear, there were big clumps of hawthorn and bramble, and in the right season we used to go there and collect pounds of blackberries. We picked them into the white pudding basin and took this home in the shopping basket: in the end, that basin held the blackberry-and-apple pudding. But right down at the bottom of the slope, far away from all the other graves, and so much in the middle of undergrowth that you couldn't see it when the trees were in leaf (though in winter you could), and after the first time my mother left me to crawl through the bushes alone to it, there was a single mound, without a stone and completely untended, that looked like an old grave. My mother was ill at ease when we found this; and (since it couldn't be the grave of a murderer, because we knew they were buried in quicklime in the gaol where they were hanged), she decided it was the grave of someone who had committed *felo-de-se*.

It was a busy day for me, because my mother never hid or hushed up anything, and so I had to learn, all at once, not only that people could be so unhappy or so ashamed that they might kill themselves, but that there was a way of doing this so much worse than the ordinary way that God would almost certainly never forgive you; and in fact, it was quite probably the 'sin against the Holy Ghost' which none of the three of us could identify with any certainty, though my mother and father were interested in it in a troubled way, and occasionally wondered whether they themselves were not guilty unawares.

My mother knew that *felo-de-se* was something extremely rare, and explained that coroners and such avoided that terrible verdict on the dead if by any means they could. She also knew that those guilty of it were buried, in principle, at the cross-roads (she didn't tell me, now I come to think of it, about driving a stake through their heart: maybe she didn't know); and would probably have thought this was still what was done. So she explained that perhaps the man's friends, or his wife, or his parents, had persuaded the cemetery people to let him be buried, at night maybe, in this overgrown and forgotten corner. I myself thought that in the dark his friends might have smuggled him over the stream by the poplars, only ten feet away, and buried him secretly in holy ground. I crept several times through the bushes to visit the *felo-de-se*. He seemed in a curious category: not a bit like burglars or murderers, or the 'bad men' I had already learnt children had to flee from. *Lost but harmless*, he was. It was odd. He might have been quite nice, though of course too sad for one to know what to do with. Still, perhaps one could have cheered him up. Then I went back, and played some more or picked the fruit.

There was a public footpath right across the sewage farm to Elmers End junction, and sometimes we walked over this, and turned left at the crossing of two broad paths in the middle of the sewage farm, and went to the big iron gates by Elmers End Road. But this path was closed to the public, and we had to turn round and come back again, because the gates—all but once—were locked. The sewage farm was full of little streams and runways, with minuscule sluice-gates to control the water. After heavy rain the streams would be noisy and turbulent, and the rank grass would be flooded. Sometimes the sewage farm smelt bad, and sometimes it smelt of fresh country air. It was always a very green place.

One couldn't turn right at the central crossing, because that went to the works, where the men were. Often you could see them, moving slowly about on the great dust-heaps. Later, an incinerator was built, and you could see its plume of smoke when it was at work. The stream between the sewage farm and the cemetery was much bigger than all the others, and always running steadily with a quite strong current: clear brown water like some mountain streams. I listened in awe to the story of a Norwood boy who had got thirsty while out playing with his friends, clambered down into the deep, broad concrete gully that stream ran in, drunk from it, and died of typhoid fever. I heard that story a lot of times, and I was frightened of that stream. But all the others I liked a lot, especially when they were rushing and gushing with the rain. We used to see lapwings and gulls on the sewage farm, and we saw these birds nowhere else, except a gull passing high overhead at home sometimes. Over the big dust-heaps the gulls were sometimes so thick that if something made them all take flight together, the air went white, you couldn't see the dust-heap through them.

Along the south-eastern edge of the sewage farm went the railway-line from Elmers End to Woodside, and beside this was a long double line of pines, and a narrow path, fenced high on both sides with wire. We called this the 'cinder-track' because it was black cinder underfoot. You could walk up this till you got right to the other side of the sewage farm, and then you could go home up the Albert Road. When I was small it seemed an immense way to cross the empty open space of the farm itself (it was about six hundred yards really) and then immense again to go all this way alongside the lines and the pine-trees. For many years, that view across the sewage farm was the widest view I knew. The pine-trees were exciting because in that open place a lot of wind could catch them, and they would toss and sweep to and fro, and make the sustained many-noted sound that a lot of pines always make. Between us and the rails ran the barbed-wire fence, the wired white gates inset at each level-crossing (there were two, but they were just for cart-tracks) and the notices warning us not to trespass, and especially not to touch the conductor-rail. Then we would see a train in the distance, small and still silent, but swaying with its own speed. It rocked and swayed all the more as it came nearer, and began its roaring noise. Then it faded and everything went quiet again, with just the pine-trees. There were steam-trains with white smoke or black, and sometimes slow goods-trains—we would hear their staggered clank-clank-clank, and the shunting noises from Elmers End yard, all the way across. Sometimes, clouds of white steam from the engines nearly reached us on the narrow shut-in cinder-track. (When a steam-engine went under the Goat House Bridge—called after a pub—back in South Norwood, two white clouds of smoke or steam used to billow up, one on each side, over the wall: and the game was to run right across before they met, swirling, in the middle.)

The electric trains were more exciting because they flashed sparks from their shoes on the conductor-rails. At night, of course, the train flashes could make big sudden sheets of light that lit up the sky a deep yellow, gone in an instant. You could see these from the other side of the sewage farm, or even, as just a fleeting light in the sky, from home sometimes. But it was on frosty and snowy days that all this was at its best. Then, when the white of the snow was weighing down the pine-branches, and the frost was already glinting everywhere, the trains would come towards us on the cinder-track with their shoes sizzling and hissing over the ice on the live rail; and there would be brilliant white or bluish flashes from them, and showers and swirls of sparks, a deep golden colour, or purple, and the clotted ice was broken and scattered by the moving shoe, to be flung off in clouds of little chips. Once or twice we saw this by night: the play of light frightened me, and made me feel the great swift power of the train.

We saw this on one of several trips which we made after dark, when I was about eight, to a house in Eden Park. I should explain that on all these walks—at least those that went across the Sewage Farm and up the cinder-track—my mother, mindful of my supposed 'weak heart', used to see that we brought the push-chair. I wheeled it for some of the time, but if I felt tired, or if she thought the time had come, I would get in and be wheeled. But on these trips we also took the push-chair because we seemed to have a lot of things to carry. Once —I forget why—my mother knew the house would be empty and decided to get it ready for when the people there got back; so we took enough kindling and coal to make a fire. I was allowed to look after the matches as a special thing; then when she thought the time had come she would get me into the push-chair, with all the odds and ends between my feet or at my side or on my knee, and would push me along.

That time we took the coal I felt, for some reason, that there was something secret about the whole expedition; though the reason why these trips were all in the dark was that we went in late afternoon or evening and it happened to be winter. The whole journey was quite a long one, rather over two miles, and it broke up in my mind into a number of clearly divided stages—in fact, into seven. First we went through the little roads near our own house, under the gas lamps and their gentle sighing sound, until by the allotments at the end of Harrington Road we could look right across the sewage farm all at once, to the lights at Elmers End, distant but bright and sharp. Then came the last gas lamps, one at the little general shop just before the cemetery gate, and the last one of all at the beginning of the sewage farm path. Now we left the metalled pavement, and went over the gravel and the bumpy stones.

It was dark across the sewage farm. In those days there were only gas lamps along the road at the side of it, and these were several hundred yards away and there weren't many of them. Once or twice it was foggy. Then, as soon as we were out on the farm, we could see nothing at all except the dark and the fog, and hear just the streams running, and the fog-signals' occasional bang. Usually my mother wheeled me this bit. The fog made our clothes damp and the arms of the push-chair wet. I sat listening to the scrunch and rattle of the wheels, and watched for a long time to see the first lamp come in a yellow blur out of the mist. This lamp was by the gate into the yard: the kind of gate that swung in a little ring of fence, to keep motor-bikes out (you could just get a push-bike through, standing it up on its back wheel: or a strong man could hoist it up and hold it flat, well above his head, and then march straight round). It took us a long time to get the push-chair through this gate, and while we did it we could hear the little whine of the gas lamp. On a clear night, from right across the sewage farm, we could watch the whole bright line of lamps along the station platform as they shone through the fir-trees, getting slowly nearer.

The next part of the walk was right round through the empty station approach, out into the road, and up the slope to the railway bridge. Now the lights were bright all round, but there would still be no one about. A steep flight of wooden steps led up to the top of the bridge, but there was another white 'kissing-gate' there, that the push-chair wouldn't go through at all; that was why we had to take the long way round.

Next, crossing the main road that ran through Elmers End village, we went, up the slope, through the estate of little grey-walled council houses behind their trim but shabby privet. We had come well over a mile now, and I remember how the rhythm of the walk would settle in. But it would be cold too. And when the council houses stopped, we had really got to the edge of London, and the country began.

Upper Elmers End Road was a broad country lane at that time, with a hedge of hawthorn and a little stream of clear water, with stickle-backs in it, all the way along on the left-hand side. Beyond the first railway bridge (they both went over the road) there were two cottages, far back from the road, on the right; and then, at the corner, the little works where they made Kempton's pies. High up on this building there was a lamp, which we could watch all the way up the dark road. I think this was the one electric lamp we saw: it ran from the pie-works' private generator. Round the corner was another little row of cottages, and the Rising Sun public house. Then, at the next corner, the first farm, with its barns and outhouses, on the left, and the next lamp, by Holly Lodge on the right. So I watched this lamp get nearer in its turn and heard its little noise, in the silence, as we passed beneath it where it lit up the holly bushes and the long oak paling of the big house.

At Holly Lodge itself there was only a slight bend, but then a new part of the walk began, and the lane ran very long and straight, with no lights at all, right up to the little general shop at Eden Park. This was the longest stretch of all. Nothing broke it up or marked it off. Usually, my mother would be pushing me by now. She just had to plod on and on, and the weak light by Mr. Marks's shop came very slowly nearer. On the foggy nights, it was a lonely part: we could see nothing save the dark for a long while. But after the shop, and the tumble-down cycle-repairer's just before it, the last bit was less lonely. To be sure, the woods on the right now drew close in to the road. But on the left came Eden Park Station, with a whole row of gas lamps; and if we had got cold we used to leave the road, walk up the steep gravel approach to the station, and go inside and get warm by the waiting-room fire. A fine bright glow that would be, and never a soul waiting by it, and the porter didn't mind. Then, when we came out, there was just the dark slope downhill again, and the second bridge where the walls were always dank and damp—sometimes running with the wet—and the last lamp showed how wet they were. It was the last one, because now we could see the street lamp outside the house we were going to. It lit up the sash window, and the young sycamore tree in the front garden. On one side, there was a pavement again. The long dark walk was over.